Project Management

A Practical Approach

Roel Grit

Third edition

Noordhoff Uitgevers Groningen|Houten

© Noordhoff Uitgevers bv

Cover design: Studio Frank & Lisa, Groningen
Cover illustration: Studio Frank & Lisa, Groningen

Translation: Prue Gargano, Fokko Veldman, Cindi Beckman, Studio Imago

If you have any comments or queries about this or any other publication, please contact: Noordhoff Uitgevers bv, Afdeling Hoger Onderwijs, Antwoordnummer 13, 9700 VB Groningen, e-mail: info@noordhoff.nl

0 1 2 3 4 5 / 15 14 13 12 11

© 2011 Noordhoff Uitgevers bv Groningen/Houten, the Netherlands

ISBN 978-90-01-79092-9
NUR 801

Foreword to the Third Edition

This book, *Project Management*, is about approaching work activities as a project. A project can be defined as a number of people working together on a temporary basis to reach a specific goal with defined resources.

More and more organizations are performing their tasks in a project-based fashion. Employees often have little experience with this type of working method. Students in higher education are being trained in project-based work approaches, often even approaching the training they provide as a project. Before a project gets under way, the project group or project team needs to put a lot of time into deciding on a uniform way of tackling the task. If this stage is rushed through, the individual project members will find themselves working in completely different ways, with inevitably unsatisfactory outcomes.

Changes from the second edition

The third edition of *Project Management* has been brought fully up to date based on user feedback. In addition to a number of textual improvements and a more attractive layout, a number of improvements have also been made to the contents:

- In the theoretical section, there is added focus on project risks, making it possible to create more a more detailed risk analysis section of the project plan.
- Considering the importance of having a good relationship with the project 'environment', a stakeholder analysis is used to devote additional attention to mapping out all those involved and communication.
- The chapter on 'Drawing up a project plan' is often used in defining a project. This chapter is included in this edition as well and a new chapter entitled 'How to carry out a project' has been added, containing practical step-by-step instructions for carrying out a project from start to finish.
- Group collaboration has become even easier these days, thanks to the variety of ICT tools available, both online and off. Instructions on using these 'virtual' tools efficiently and effectively within a project group have been added to this edition.
- To prevent the book from becoming too cumbersome, the chapters on 'Making an offer' and 'Writing letters' have been omitted. If you still require this information, these two sections can be downloaded free of charge (by book owners) from the website.
- A number of textual changes have also been made for reasons of clarity, the most important being that the term 'project assignment' has been replaced with 'project result' and term 'intermediate product' is now 'intermediate result'.

Website www.projectmanagement-english.noordhoff.nl
- A number of the checklists that can be downloaded from the website and the MS Word and MS Excel models have been expanded.

- Tests for students and online lectures for students have been added to the website.
- The website also contains cases and an exam database for instructors.

The website accompanying this book is extremely popular. The book therefore makes clear reference to the website where relevant. This is shown in the text using the icon shown here. More detailed information on the contents of the website can be found in Appendix 2.

Who is this book for?

This book was originally written for students at institutes of higher learning and universities, though it is also a practical tool for use in non-educational organisations. It was written as a practical introduction to working on projects. More and more students of higher education are being lectured on the theoretical backgrounds of project management. This book emphasizes the practical aspects, not the theory. The central theme here is "How do you do that in practice?" The imperative voice (commanding) is therefore used in Section 2 of this book.

Project management in education

It is becoming increasingly more common in education to use a project-based approach in preparing for practical application. This includes detailed study assignments, internal projects, internship projects and thesis projects. A thesis project can – and perhaps should be – approached as a project.
In higher vocational education and at universities, Section 1 can be covered during a number of classes or lectures. In doing so, it is important that the philosophy behind a project-based approach is emphasised to students. In this instance, the instructor is more of an inspirer and motivator than a teacher.
Groups of two to three students can be formed and given the assignment of drawing up a project plan and management summary based on a small case. Assignments formulated for this purpose can be found at the back of this book. These have been tested extensively in an educational setting. Alternatively or additionally, small groups of students can carry out a 'real' project assignment. If none is available, a detailed case can be used. Several cases

are available on the website. The instructor can take on the role of sponsor, while the other students and/or other instructors can provide expertise on the subject matter. However, a 'real' assignment, whether within or outside of the organisation, is more realistic and therefore preferable. The assignment should be carried out based on interviews with the sponsor or others and concretized in a project plan.
To practice project skills as effectively as possible, a large project group can also be formed. Because of its size, it will be necessary to allocate group tasks, while the supervisor of the group dictates which tools and techniques from this book are to be used: setting up a project, holding a meeting, drawing up a schedule, presenting the results and so on. See the relevant chapters on tools in the second section, as well as Integration Assignment 3 at the back of the book. In this case, the supervisor takes on the role of 'manager of the educational process', rather than instructor. This book makes it much easier for the supervisor to monitor the quality of the project.

Roel Grit
Emmen, Spring 2011
www.roelgrit.nl

Contents

Website www.projectmanagement-english.noordhoff.nl

Additional materials:
Writing letters
Making a project offer

Downloadable tools:	*Chapter*
Sample schedule and MS Project (zipped)	4
PowerPoint presentation for Chapter 4	4
Spartavus case (for making a project plan)	5
Amalia Hospital case (for making a project plan)	5
DropCo case (for making a project plan)	5
Writing letters	6
Making a project offer	6
Agenda model	6
Minutes model	6
Sample project proposal	6
Sample project progress report	6
Sample weekly report	6
Initial interview checklist	6
Presentation checklist	6
Mini-Course on MS Project	6
Sample plan of approach	4, 5, 6
Sample planning	5, 6
Sample risk analysis (by Jurgen Winkel)	5, 6
Stakeholder analysis checklist	5, 6
Sample information matrix	5, 6
Time registration 1 model	5, 6
Time registration 2 model	5, 6
Practice tests	1, 2, 3, 4
Online lectures	some

Introduction

Structure of this book

The aim of this book is to provide those with little experience in working in a project-based manner the theory they need to do so. It also describes a number of practical tools for approaching project-based work activities.

Project Management consists of three parts:
- Part 1 of this book: Practical Theory
- Part 2 of this book: Project Tools
- Website: www.projectmanagement-english.noordhoff.nl

The structure of Project Management

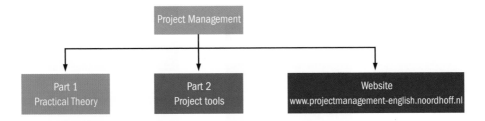

Part 1   Practical Theory

The first four chapters contain a short theoretical background to working in a project-based manner. This section describes what a project-based approach entails, when it is appropriate to take such an approach and how to make it work. Chapter 4 deals with the scheduling of activities.

Part 2   Project Tools

The second section of this book describes a number of the practical tools and skills needed to tackle projects, including how to organize and hold a project meeting, how to make an executive summary and how to write a report. An important aspect of the early stages of a project – drawing up a project plan – is dealt with in Chapter 5 and Chapter 6, which explains how to approach a project in a step-by-step fashion.

A number of the skills that are dealt with in this section – organizing meetings, writing reports and holding presentations, for instance – are also useful in contexts other than those described here.

Website

There is a detailed website with a range of different tools accompanying this book (www.projectmanagement-english.noordhoff.nl).

Appendix 2 provides detailed information on the contents of the website. Two chapters can also be downloaded from the website that were omitted from this most recent edition of the book.

The structure of Project Management

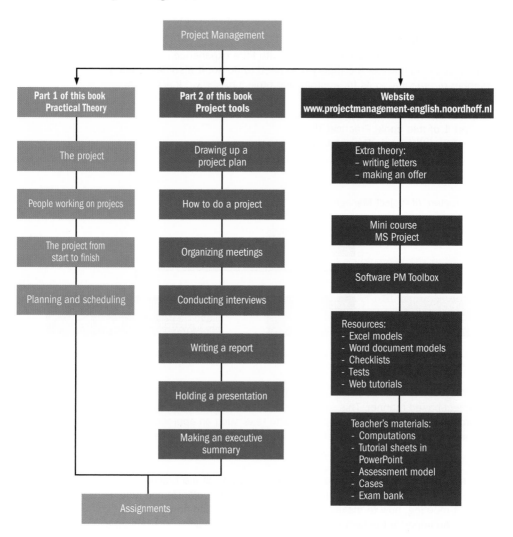

Theoretically, there is nothing particularly difficult about project management. Projects nevertheless frequently fail to attain their objectives. Since
project work is very dependent on the people involved in it, those involved
need to be aware of the fact that there is a difference between ordinary
ways of approaching work and working in a project-based manner. This
section of the book deals with the theory underlying the project-based
approach to work based on real-life situations.

The following questions will be addressed in this part:
• What is the difference between project-based work and other work?
• How do I organize the project?
• How do I start the project?
• How do I monitor the project?
• How do I plan the project?

PART 1

Practical Theory

project

1
The project

Jobs for life are a thing of the past. With our society caught up in a process of constant change, organizations are finding that they have to both respond to each change while already anticipating the next one. Their responses often take the form of projects. Being able to manage projects effectively has therefore become a necessity. The important issues are not only when to take a project-based approach and how to tackle the project itself, but even what a project actually is.

This chapter describes how project-based work differs from 'regular' work.

1.1 Types of activities, types of work

All kinds of activities take place within an organization. They may be characterized in the following three groups of activities:

Three groups of activities

1 Improvised activities
2 Routine activities
3 Project-based activities

This book deals with the last type. To show the special position that project-based activities occupy, all three types of activity will be described.

Improvised activities

Improvised work

Ad hoc

An *improvised work* approach to new activities is one option. People usually improvise when something unforeseen that requires an immediate response occurs. Their reaction will be an *ad hoc* one: not according to a laid down plan, but decided on as events unfold.

Since there are no directions about what to do that can be given beforehand, it is hard to predict with any accuracy the outcomes of working in an ad hoc manner. The advantage of not having any directions is that the new situations can be met in a flexible manner. However, while the large amount of freedom may be welcomed by the improviser, it carries the risk of chaos and could put the organization under a lot of pressure. Workers in an organization in which there is a lot of improvisation going on are likely to be working under a certain amount of strain. Having to constantly adjust to changing working conditions is, after all, quite stressful.

Routine activities

Routine

Routine activities are activities that are repeated frequently and are relatively predictable. The work will be carried out according to predetermined patterns. Since there is a precedent, it is not necessary to constantly think about what has to be done next.

Work procedures

In order to be able to perform these routine activities efficiently, *work procedures* or instructions have to be developed. Most of the activities carried out within an organization belong to this type. Production line activities, sales procedures, purchasing procedures and administrative activities are some examples.

Project-based activities

Project-based activities fall roughly midway between improvised and routine activities. They are non-recurring and have a limited duration, but are reasonably predictable.

According to a plan

In order to increase this predictability, the work should be done *according to a plan*. Plans gradually illuminate each phase of the process. Before the activities get underway, some time needs to be spent on working out what the aims are and how to achieve them.

Phases

Project plan

For this to be effective, large projects are often divided up into a number of *phases*. After each of these phases, the aims and procedures may be adjusted. Before starting the project, a *project plan* is formulated, the instructions for which are given in Chapter 6. By working with a project plan based on fixed criteria, some degree of routine can be introduced to the project. In other words, 'You introduce routine to something you have never done before'. This greatly enhances the possibility of success.

Project organization

Projects often have an organization of their own, one created specially to deal with the needs of the project. People who do not normally work together may do so as part of the project group. Each will have their own specific tasks.

Some of the activities of businesses such as shipbuilding, aircraft construction and information technology are regularly carried out as project-based activities. In other businesses, project-based activities may be the exception rather than the rule. Such a project might involve a departmental reorganization, moving into new quarters, or the introduction of a new computer network.

A project-based activity is not an objective in itself, of course. It is a way of structuring activities that are less predictable than others and that fall outside the scope of normal activities. These structured activities then become easier to manage and monitor.

Table 1.1 contains a summary of the properties of the various types of activities.

TABLE 1.1 Types of activities

	Improvised	Project-based	Routine
When?	Ad hoc (suddenly)	Predictable	Repetitive
Result?	Uncertain	Reasonably certain	Certain
Familiarity?	New, sudden	New, planned	Well-known
Freedom?	A lot of freedom	A suitable amount	Little freedom
Procedures?	Chaotic	Increasingly clear	Clear

1.2 Examples of projects

The following overview gives a number of examples of projects. The website accompanying this book (www.projectmanagement-english.noordhoff.nl) contains further examples.
- Building a new shopping centre, bridge, housing estate, nursing home or factory
- The technical development of a new product such as an electric razor, a computer or a car
- Developing a marketing plan or export plan for a new product like the iPad
- Reducing waiting lists in the field of healthcare
- Designing a new school course
- Formulating an information plan, sales plan, personnel plan or training plan
- Doing a theatre production such as *"We Will Rock You"* or producing a feature film or information film
- Doing the research for a thesis
- Developing a new house style for an organization
- Organizing a major exhibition such as a retrospective on Rembrandt

- Organizing a major event like Pink Pop, a major sports event or home fair
- Implementing a large-scale software package at an organization, such as financial software, logistics software, client management software or patient information system
- Setting up a website for an organization such as a hospital or commercial business
- Arranging a logistical system for providing meals in a hospital
- Adjusting a company's logistics in response to engaging in e-commerce
- Reducing the total drug expenses at a hospital
- Developing a project to improve communication between the hospital and family doctors
- Relocating a large company to a new location

Projects are not a modern trend.
- Ancient Egypt's biggest projects – building the pharaohs' pyramids – were even started during the lifetime of each pharaoh.
- Wars required a project-based approach even in times past. During a long campaign, the logistics of a large army demanded a lot of preparation. Napoleon was a great general because he was an excellent project manager!
- Columbus' preparations for his 1492 journey to America are a masterly example of project management. He was not as successful in executing his plans, however: India, and not America, was his destination.

1.3 What is a project?

This book is about project management, but what exactly is a project?

> A project can be defined as a group of people, usually from various fields of expertise, collaborating temporarily with the aim of reaching a predetermined goal within a predetermined budget.

Features of a project

A project should have the following features:
- A project should have a clear starting point, known as the project *start-up* or kick-off.
- Because a project has a **limited duration**, a finishing date needs to be set.
- A project has a *unique* and clearly **defined goal**. The project's outcome is the end product. This could be a variety of things, such as a new machine, building, report or even an event.
- The project goal tells why the sponsor has commissioned the project. The project result is the outcome of the project and contributes to the project goal.
- A project (usually) has a "**client**" who has commissioned the project and who pays for the project, commonly referred to as the "**sponsor**". This is the person who has an interest in the project result, provide the project team with clarity on the project and make important decisions.
- A project has a **budget** that needs to be determined in advance. The project group has to make do with that amount. The budget consists of money for funding the project and paying the project's staff. A project without a financial budget should at least have a time budget applicable to those participating in the project.
- The project group usually consists of people from **various fields** of expertise working together as a temporary team. The members of the project

may come from various parts of the organization and have their own particular skills. They include managers, financial experts, economists, marketing experts and technicians. Each is familiar with the terminology of his or her own field and has his or her own perspective on things. This makes working on a project both interesting and challenging.

- A project has its own **organizational set-up**. An employee who is temporarily relieved of his normal duties to take part in a project will suddenly have a different person to be accountable to: the project manager. The person (or body) the project manager is accountable to is the sponsor.
- A project is initiated as a purposeful move. It *never* starts *spontaneously*. It has to be initiated and organized consciously. The sponsor appoints a project manager with sufficient authority and the capacities to give shape to the project. The project manager then draws up a *project plan* in consultation with the sponsor. This project plan describes the project in detail. Chapter 5 explains how to draw up a project plan.

Never spontaneously

Since the members of the project team have to work together, they have to know what is expected of them. They must make mutual arrangements about such things as the resources to be used and where the meetings will be held. These are only a few of the matters that need to be arranged. It is also essential that all members of the project team be able to work in a *result-oriented fashion*. After all, the goal is to achieve the project results!

Result-oriented fashion

1.4 From improvised activities to project to routine

Improvised activities, project-based activities and routine work can be part of the same work sequence. There is likely to be a lot of initial improvisation when an organization takes on a new task. As soon as it becomes obvious that the task will have to be repeated, a greater degree of organization will become necessary. A project whose aim is to put things on the rails properly could then be undertaken. By the end of the project, standard working procedures will have been developed. Improvisation will be a thing of the past; the activities can now be carried out as the standard routine. Figure 1.1 shows this process as a diagram.

FIGURE 1.1 From improvised activities to routine

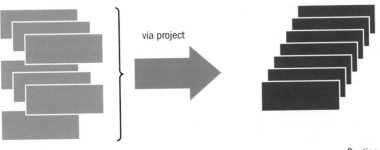

via project

Improvisation

Routine

1.5 Types of projects

According to their character, projects fall into one of several different categories: technical projects, social projects, commercial projects, mixed projects and events.

Technical projects

Technical projects are projects whose aim it is to effect some change in technology or to come up with a new product. These projects are usually relatively easy to plan. The end result is usually obvious. The construction of a building, a bridge, a road, a pipeline or a railway line are some such projects. These projects are also known as "hard" projects.

Social projects

The outcomes of *social projects* are usually not quite as evident. In the business arena, their aim is very often to change the corporate culture or organizational structure of a company. They deal with the way in which people work together. Because people tend to resist changes, social projects are more difficult to execute than technical projects. Social projects include a reorganization of a firm or an adaptation of work procedures. Social projects are also known as "soft" projects.

Commercial projects

The ultimate goal of *commercial projects* is to earn money. Examples are conducting market research, developing a new product or introducing a new product on the market.

Mixed projects

Mixed projects combine some of the aspects of both technical and social projects. The design, programming and installation of an extensive computer program is an example of a mixed project. These kinds of projects can be especially complicated since the members of the project team come from a wide variety of areas of expertise and do not always "speak each other's language".

Events are a special kind of project, as the end result only appears at a certain point in time. Examples of events are a computer fair, pop festival, home fair or car show.

Projects can also be categorized in different ways based on content, such as those with an internal sponsor as opposed to those with an external sponsor. Another possibility is to categorize projects into those that provide a service (course, event) and those that yield a "product" (building, railway line).

1.6 Things to remember

Later in the book an entire chapter will be devoted to scheduling and organizing a project. This section will describe a few of the basic principles.

If you are the manager of a project, there are a number of things you will have to keep in mind. These are discussed below.

Request planning time from the sponsor

Systematism
Decision-making

To *work systematically*, a project plan is essential. Make sure that the sponsor allows enough time for planning the project. The *decision-making process* can slow things down considerably, especially in large organizati-

ons. It could be weeks or even months before the definitive project comes up for discussion and is approved. When you draw up your schedules, you should allow for the time needed to get the project approved. If not, you will have to deal with delays even before your project gets underway!
In a small organization, the opposite might be the case. People are often asked to start immediately. Nobody should expect a project manager to embark instantly on a task that has never been done before.

Consult everyone involved
Since there are likely to be people from various fields of expertise working together on the project, it is imperative that the project be talked over with all parties involved. Make sure you have enough enthusiastic people and enough funds for the project. Make good arrangements about the contribution expected of every worker.
Mistakes made in the early stages of the project are best rectified there   **Mistakes**
and then. If not, the team's hardworking members may find that the work they have done has been for nothing. At the beginning of a project a mistake can usually be easily rectified, whereas later on in the project it might take ten times as long to do so.
A word of warning: if you think that a project is doomed from the start, you should make sure that you are not the project manager!

Work from the top down
Set out the main lines of the project first. Avoid getting bogged down in details: they should be dealt with later on. However enticing it may be to commence with the more minor aspects of the project, make sure you avoid doing this. You may find that you have lost sight of the whole. Dividing a project into *phases* is one way of keeping it manageable. Projects can   **Phases**
generally be divided into the following phases (Figure 1.2):
- Preparation (think)
- Execution (act)
- Aftercare (maintain)

These phases will be described in detail in the following section.

FIGURE 1.2 The phases of a small project

Thinking things through: from start to finish and from finish to start
As the definition suggests, project work is work on a new situation. As such, you cannot rely on your experience. You need to determine what exactly needs to take place when carrying out the project. It is important not to overlook a single activity because your schedules will otherwise not be reliable.

It is also important to look at a project from two directions: from start to finish as well as from finish to start. When a new bridge is built, it is not only the initial steps that need to be thought through. The official opening of the bridge by the queen's representative needs to be thought through too. There may be tasks associated with the concluding stages that could easily be overlooked. Remember: if you overlook it in the beginning stages, it will return with a vengeance later on!

1.7 Doing things in phases

To manage

It is often difficult *to manage* large projects. Staying within the budget, getting the job finished by the deadline, and achieving the project result can all present problems. It is the task of the sponsor to ensure that the project is manageable. Projects such as the Channel tunnel between England and France and the Dutch land reclamation scheme were difficult to manage. On the whole, long-term projects are more difficult to manage than short-term ones. This is understandable in light of the changes constantly taking place within the world. The longer a project lasts, the more chance there is that the aims and goals of the project will have to be adjusted.

Project plan

There are a number of measures that can be taken to keep a project manageable. First, a project plan (*plan of approach*) should be made at the commencement of the project. This should contain a clear description of the project. It should also describe the project's objectives and the desired end products, and show the available funds and the schedules for the activities (see Chapter 5).

Phases

A large project is often divided into a number of *phases*. Each phase will, naturally, be shorter in duration than the project as a whole. A phase can be regarded as a series of project activities that have a logical connection to each other. Phasing minimizes the risks associated with the project.

The following are some common and useful project phases:
- *Concept*: the idea that sparks it off. The concept phase of a project often results in a *project proposal*. If the proposal is approved by management (the sponsor), the next phase may commence.
- *Definition*: defining the end result of the project and what needs to be done to achieve it. The result of the definition is a *project plan*. With complicated projects, it is common to carry out various **sub-projects**, each with its own project plan.
- *Design*: deciding what the project result will be, i.e. "how to go about it". What will the sponsor be getting for his money? This phase results in the design report.
- *Preparation*: detailing how to do it. This phase results in a detailed design, such as a building plan.
- *Execution*: doing it. This phase results in the end result desired by the sponsor.
- *Aftercare*: making it operational and providing aftercare. The result is maintained by adapting it to new desires and resolving any problems.

Figure 1.3 summarizes the above.

FIGURE 1.3 Phasing and the products of every phase

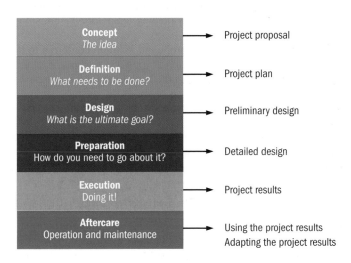

The various phases will now be described. Each phase will be illustrated using a concrete example: building a house (a technical project).

Concept
At this stage, the project exists only as a problem or an idea in the minds   **Idea**
of those who have thought it up. They (the project's initiators) believe that
something needs to be undertaken. If a decision to proceed is made at the
managerial level, a number of activities may be carried out:
• An investigation into the current state of affairs
• A rough estimation of the extent of the problem
• A determination of the aims or the desired results of the project
• A determination of the feasibility of the project. If desired, a feasibility
  study or a *preliminary investigation* could be carried out.

This phase could result in an authorized commission or project proposal in   **Project**
which the sponsor gives the go ahead for starting the project. Alternatively,   **proposal**
it could be decided not to take any further action and to let the matter rest.

Definition
The project's objectives emerge during the definition phase. The project has
been given a fiat; the desired objectives must now be established. It is
important to make a distinction between the project's *formal objectives* and   **Formal**
the *wishes* of those involved. The project's objectives have to be met: this is   **objectives**
mandatory. It is desirable that the wishes of those concerned be met, but   **Wishes**
there is no necessity about this. At the conclusion of the definition phase
there should be a project plan in which the project is defined in detail. (The
drawing up of a *project plan* is the subject of Chapter 5.) By the end of the   **Project plan**
definition phase there needs to be an answer to the following question:
what will have been achieved when the project has been completed?

Design

The definition phase establishes what the project's objectives are. During the design phase, a way of resolving the problem has to be found. If the project is building a house, it is during this phase that a detailed construction drawing is made. This phase makes a demand on the creativity of the

Brainstorming sessions

participants. It can be stimulated by holding *brainstorming* sessions with all the participants.

In order to determine whether the proposed solution conforms to the requirements as laid down, one option is to make a *prototype* of it.

Prototype

A prototype is a simplified version of the real thing, and it can be used to test the demands that are likely to be made of the design. For instance, when a new airplane is being designed, the prototype's properties are tested in a wind tunnel.

Design

At the end of this phase, there should be a *design* that does the following:
- Shows the sponsor exactly what he will be getting
- Shows those who will be actively involved in the next phase exactly what has to be produced.

Preparation

During the preparation phase, the design that was prepared during the previous phase is made ready for production. Attention is now focused on how the design can be produced. This could take the form of a detailed construction drawing that shows a metal worker exactly how to make a certain part, or assembly instructions showing exactly how certain parts should be fitted together. The product itself is not produced during this phase. The aim is to create the conditions to allow the production phase to take place without a hitch. The motto of this phase is look before you leap.

Execution

After all the preliminaries, the actual work can now get underway. Depending on how thorough the preliminaries have been, there will be a proportionally less risk of unpleasant surprises during the production phase. During this phase, the objectives of the project are achieved and the product constructed. It does not necessarily have to be a technical product such as a machine: it could also be the reorganization of a factory or the introduction of a new system for production planning.

Implementation

This phase is also the phase of *implementation*. Measures have to be taken to facilitate the introduction of the project's outcomes. In the case of a transition from an old to a new situation, these will take the form of

Conversion measures

conversion measures. If the project involves making a new computer program for the computerization of a production process, the employees will have to be trained to work with the program. When a manual system of personnel administration is computerized, all the personnel data will have

Project's outcomes

to be fed into the computer. At the end of this phase the *project's outcomes* are delivered.

Aftercare

In the aftercare phase the project's outcomes are put to use. Because circumstances alter as time goes on, the demands that are made of the products are likely to change as well. This may require making some adjustments to them. The finished products will also require aftercare. In the case of a technical project such as the building of a bridge, the aftercare should be provided by a maintenance crew set up for that purpose. In the case of a computerization project, any change in circumstances will mean that the program has to be updated. In short, after the project is finished the job is not yet over. It is important not to underestimate this phase. The costs associated with maintenance can sometimes be many times greater than the cost of the project itself.

1.8 Why do things in phases?

Executing a large project in phases has the advantage that a *number of opportunities for decision making* are built into the project. At the end of each phase the sponsor has an opportunity to alter the project. The options available are as follows:

Number of opportunities for decision making

- Continue as planned
- Continue with some alterations to the project
- Termination of the project

To terminate a project requires a great deal of courage. After all, a lot of time and effort has already been invested in it. The benefits must outweigh the costs during every phase of the project. The amount already invested in the project should not be an argument to continue. If continuing the project has already cost half a million and another $400,000 is still needed, then arguing that we cannot stop now makes no sense if the benefits of the project will only be $300,000. Also see section 3.12.

1.9 The phases of a project: an illustration

In building a house, we might come across the phasing process mentioned above. We use a detailed example to indicate the types of activities that take place during every phase.

Concept
A family with two children lives in a village in the countryside. The husband is a lecturer in a large city relatively close by; the children have reached the age of attending secondary school in the large city. The husband is fed up with being caught up in traffic jams before he gets to work every morning. Since they have inherited quite a large amount of money from an unexpected source, they could have a house built in a new housing estate on the outskirts of the city. They contact a real estate agent to investigate the possibilities.

Definition
The real estate agent and the couple look into a number of things:
- The financial possibilities. How much money does the couple have, what is the family's income and how much money could they borrow to build the house/how much money do they want to borrow?
- The availability of a suitable piece of land to build on. What are the municipal regulations relating to building a house?
- What sort of house they want. This family wants four bedrooms, a large living room, a garage and a large backyard.

After the couple has made up their mind, they and the real estate agent go looking for an architect to draw up a plan for the house.

Design

The list of requirements is talked through with the architect. On the basis of this the architect does some drawings of the new house: the design. While he is working on the drawings he frequently consults the couple about various details: for example, the colour of the bathroom tiles and where to put the power points in the living room. The house design as well as a description of how it will fulfil all the requirements, budgetary and otherwise, is eventually ready. The drawings should give the future owners a clear picture of what the house they are commissioning will be like.

Preparation

On the basis of the drawings, additional technical drawings are made. The drawing of the electrical wiring will show the electrician exactly where to put the cables during the construction of the house. Drawings are also made of the sewerage system and the water and gas pipes. The capacity of the central heating system and the radiators is calculated. The drawings will give the builders and contractors of the next phase exact instructions on how to proceed. Now a building contractor needs to be found to do the actual building of the house.

Execution

The building contractor makes a plan for the building of the house. Various tradesmen will be needed: bricklayers, carpenters, electricians and plumbers, for example. The technical drawings from the previous phase serve as a blueprint for the construction of the house. At the end of this phase the house is ready and the family can move from their old home to their new one. In a sense, moving house is the *conversion* from the old situation to the new.

Conversion

Aftercare

After the new owners have been living in the new house for a while – putting the outcomes of the project to use – they will have to make sure the house is maintained. The woodwork will have to be painted, the backyard landscaped and any necessary repairs done (a door repaired, for example). Because the husband is now spending more time working from home and he cannot do so with adolescents around him all the time, they decide to have an extra study attached to the house. All these activities are aimed at maintaining the project's outcomes and adjusting them to changing circumstances.

1.10 When to do it as a project

You are probably expecting a book on project management to recommend adopting a project-based approach. But that is not the case here. There are certainly advantages to a project-based approach, but naturally also disadvantages.

Advantages of a project-based approach

There are a number of advantages to a project-based approach:
- The project is not part of your everyday work; time has been set aside especially for the project.
- Since the members of the project team are able to concentrate on the project at hand, there is a greater chance of better results.

- There is a sponsor for the project who can make decisions when necessary.
- If there is a clear project plan (see Chapter 5), all parties involved will know exactly what must be done.
- The responsibilities of the project manager, sponsor and members of the project team are clearly defined in the project plan.
- If project is to be carried out in phases, it will be well organized.
- If the project team is well chosen, the members will complement and support one another, thereby increasing the productivity of every member.
- Since a project is started in order to achieve a specific end result, there is a smaller risk of failure.
- Working in a project team is a valuable experience and enables the members of the project team to develop and perhaps later on serve in a management position.

Disadvantages of a project-based approach
There are also a number of disadvantages to a project-based approach:
- Setting up and organizing a project costs time.
- A variety of individuals must be consulted and a project team has to be put together. It also takes time to formulate a good project plan.
- Since members of a particular department take part in the project, they leave behind a "gap" in their department that must be filled.
- A project-based approach can also be complicated. Inexperienced members of the project team sometimes must be trained first.
- Although the project team learns from the experience, it has less of an effect outside of the group since the most complicated tasks are carried out within a limited project group.

When should a project-based approach be used?
It is relatively time-consuming to set up a project organization for a rather minor "job". For example, if this "job" can be carried out in only a week's time, it would be unwise to use a project-based approach. A good rule of thumb is to only use a project-based approach if the duration of the project is at least two to three months. However, if a project is expected to take a year, it is worth considering whether it would not be better to divide it into several sub-projects.

1.11 Lifecycle of a project

The goal of a project is to achieve a specific goal. However, the end result is often only temporary. The results of reorganizing a car factory or manu-facturing a new car model, for instance, will lose their value in the long term. After a number of years, the car factory will start up a new project in order to manufacture an even newer car model. The entire process from start to finish of a project is called the "project *lifecycle*". Figure 1.4 illustrates this.

Lifecycle

FIGURE 1.4 Lifecycle of a project

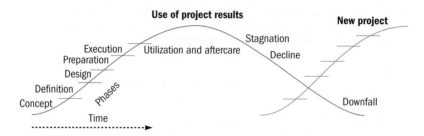

You can recognize the phases of concept, definition, preliminary design, detailed design and production at the start of the project. At the end of the production phase, the end result is accomplished and subsequently used.

Utilization   This latter phase is also called "*utilization*". During the utilization of the project result, aftercare and maintenance are required to maintain the results and keep them up to date. After some time, aftercare might be insufficient and stagnation will occur. With the case of the car factory mentioned above, for example, sales of the model start slowing down or the factory becomes obsolete from a technical perspective. A decline then follows and the project result is no longer useful. In the meantime, a new project might be started up to manufacture an even new car model or build a new factory, and the lifecycle of a new project begins.

1.12 Project goals should be SMART

Projects are carried out in order to achieve a certain goal. It is therefore important to examine ways in which goals can best be described. Project

SMART   goals should be defined using the SMART principle. SMART stands for:
- Specific
- Measurable
- Acceptable
- Realistic
- Time-bound

Specific
The project goal must be specific, i.e. described in detail. In other words, what exactly are we going to do? There should be no misunderstanding as to the end result. For example, "We're going to improve the delivery of our products" is not specific enough. More specific would be to say "We need to shorten the delivery time for our products".

Measurable
The goal must be measurable. This means that it should be possible afterwards to determine whether the project goal has been reached (or not) with regard to time, money, quality and quantity. Measurability is also important for determining when the goal is actually reached: When am I finished? For example, "The delivery time of our products must be reduced from five to two days."

1

Acceptable

A person or group must be responsible for achieving the goal. So who will that be? The goal must also be acceptable for the person who must achieve it. For example, "The Logistics Department must reduce the delivery time of our product from five to two days."

Realistic

The goal must be feasible and realistic. Can we achieve this goal? If the goal is not realistic, the project members will have little interest in pursuing it and will quit. For example, "The Logistics Department must reduce the delivery time of our product from five to *three* days" (since "two days" was not realistic).

Time-bound

There is a specific deadline by which the goal must be achieved. For example, "The Logistics Department must reduce the delivery time of our products from five to two days by December 31 of this year."

The following are two examples in which goals have been defined according to the SMART principle.

EXAMPLE 1.1

A personal goal

The goal "I want to live a healthier lifestyle" defined according to the SMART principle: "I (A) want to lose (S) five pounds (M) over the next three months (T)." The feasibility (R) of losing five pounds in three months is for you to determine.

EXAMPLE 1.2

A project goal

The goal of reducing waiting lists: "The Surgery Unit (A) must reduce (M and R) the waiting lists for hip operations (S) by 20% by December 31 of this year (T)."

1.13 Carrying out the projects in this book

This chapter provides a brief introduction to project management. A more detailed theoretical explanation of project management can be found in the following three chapters:
- Chapter 2 People working on projects
- Chapter 3 The project from start to finish
- Chapter 4 Planning and scheduling

The second half of this book contains a number of practical tools, such as how to formulate a project plan, step-by-step instructions for carrying out a project, how to hold a project meeting and how to present the end result. To properly understand project management, it is advisable to closely read through the first four chapters of this book before getting started. But if you are eager to get started right away, you can begin directly by formulating a project plan (Chapter 5). The project plan is used to define the project before you begin carrying it out.

If you want to carry out a project from the very first step to the very last, it is best to start with Chapter 6 "Carrying out a project". This chapter cleans clear-cut practical steps – divided into activities – that take you through this process. This step-by-step plan refers to Chapter 5 on drawing up a project plan.

Figure 1.5 below provides an overview of the process (with the chapter numbers between brackets) that can be used to carry out a project from start to finish.

FIGURE 1.5 This book and carrying out a project

Project start-up	Project execution	Project completion
• Theoretical preparation (1, 2, 3)	• Carrying out a project (6)	• Carrying out a project (6)
• Carrying out a project (6)	• Execution and mastery (3)	• Writing reports (9)
• Interviewing (8)	• Updating the planning	• Presenting the end result (10)
• Drawing up a project plan (5)	(4, website)	• Writing a management summary
• Project start-up (3)	• Meeting (7)	(11)
• Initial planning (4, 5, website)	• Interviewing (8)	
• Making a project offer (website)	• Presenting the intermediate results (10)	
	• Writing letters (website)	

Assignments

1.1 a For which of the three groups of activity that have been mentioned in this chapter is it possible to draw up working procedures?
   b Give three examples of situations where activities could be carried out in an improvised manner.
   c Give three examples of routine work.
   d A vacation can be approached in a routine, improvised or project-based manner. Give an example of each.

1.2 a Which six phases in the execution of a large-scale project are used in this book?
   b Describe in your own words the contents of each of these phases.
   c Which phases can be combined for a small project?
   d Explain why projects are broken down into phases.
   e Why should a project not take too long?

1.3 Name three projects in your own area of expertise.

1.4 a Define a project.
   b Which persons participate in a project and what are their roles?

1.5 Explain the following statement: "Improvisation can be turned into routine using a project-based approach."

1.6 What are the different types of projects? Explain which type you believe is the most difficult to carry out.

1.7 a Why is it advisable to work from the top down?
   b What does "Projects are sometimes difficult to manage" mean?

1.8 In which phase of a project do the following belong?
   a Design report
   b Project plan
   c Building plans
   d Project proposal
   e Project result

1.9 Suppose someone wants to start a copying company.
   a Which phases would you recommend?
   b List a number of activities for every phase.

1.10   Large "jobs" are not always carried out as projects.
   a List three advantages of a project-based approach.
   b List three disadvantages of a project-based approach.

1.11   Describe the following goals using the SMART principle:
   a I want to be a journalist.
   b I want to use my time better.
   c I want to be a better student.
   d The cafeteria needs updating.
   e I want to improve my relationship with my sponsor.
   f The communication in my project group must be improved.

1.12   What is meant by:
   a A discipline
   b Brainstorming;
   c A prototype
   d The implementation of a project
   e Conversion
   f A project plan

1.13   This assignment should be done in groups. Each group is assigned to list
   as many activities associated with the following projects as possible:
   a Organizing a big party
   b Organizing an excursion to Brussels
   c Putting a new product on the market
   d Computerizing the financial administration system
   e Designing a mould

   The various groups work on the same assignment should then compare
   their results, paying special attention to the differences between them.

1.14   Should a final thesis project for an institute for higher professional education be regarded as a project? Comment.

1.15   Explain why projects are being carried out more frequently now than in the
   past.

1.16   a Chose five of the examples given in section 1.2. Ask your trainer or teacher
      for assistance if necessary.
   b Give a clear description of the outcomes of each of these projects.
   c Compare your answers to **b** with those of someone who has chosen the
      same examples.

1.17   Clothing manufacturer X is not doing well.
   a List three possible causes.
   b For every cause, come up with a project that could resolve or turn around
      the problem.

1.18   Company Y never works with projects. Explain step by step how the
   company can implement a project-based approach.

1.19   Discuss the following statements in groups:
- **a** Working in a project-like way is a trend that is likely to be short-lived.
- **b** Devising a project plan takes up a lot of time and is better left out, especially if it is a small project.
- **c** You cannot terminate a project that has already had 100,000 dollars invested in it.
- **d** Routine work makes you unhappy.
- **e** Working together in a project is a good opportunity to develop your own capacities.
- **f** Carrying out a project in phases is not always necessary.

project

2
People working on projects

In a rapidly changing world, companies are finding that they have to adapt their products on an ongoing basis. Many customers are no longer satisfied with standard products: they want products made to suit their own needs and specifications. This forces organizations to change their structures more frequently than they used to. It also means that people within these organizations have to collaborate with different people all the time.

This chapter talks about different types of organizations, leadership and the roles played by employees.

2.1 Line organization

Organization chart

Companies are organized in different ways. A good way to clarify the organizational method is to draw an organizational chart. An *organization chart* is a diagram that includes all departments within an organization and the balance of power between them. See Figure 2.1.

FIGURE 2.1 Line organization with staff department

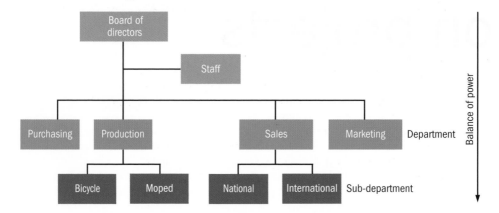

Figure 2.1 shows an organizational chart for a bicycle factory. A distinction is made between the line and staff departments. There is a balance of power among the *line departments* – along the "line" from top to bottom. The departmental manager is also the head of the sub-departments. The manager of the Production Department, for example, is also the boss of the manager of the Bicycle Department.

Line department

Staff department

A *staff department* (such as Human Resources or Administrative Department) usually provides advice or support, but does not have the power to command other departments. In the organizational chart shown here, the staff departments are drawn next to the "line". However, the employees of a staff department are referred to as staff officers.

2.2 The project organization

In order to carry out a project, management must establish a separate project organization. This organization is "outside" of the normal line organization (see Figure 2.2) and has its own, temporary project manager, who acts as the temporary manager of the members of the project team. This section discusses all possible "parties" within a project organization.

FIGURE 2.2 A project is separate from the line organization

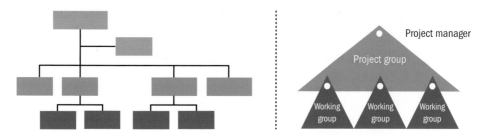

2

The project group
A project group is made up of people who have been brought together because of their particular capacities, expertise and aptitude. To weld the group into a team, a good, positive atmosphere is essential: the members of the group may not even know each other.
Despite the fact that the work a project group does is often done under pressure, many people find working together in a group a pleasurable experience. One of the positive aspects of a project is that the main organization very often pays it extra attention, thereby giving the project members greater status.

As well as setting out the tasks of each individual in the team, the team has to make decisions relating to how its members should collaborate, how and when meetings are scheduled, and how decisions are reached.

A project group performs several functions:
- **Project management** is the task of the project manager. A larger project may be divided up into various working groups with a working group manager in charge of each. A project manager is sometimes supported by an assistant project manager. The tasks of a project manager will be dealt with in greater detail in section 2.5.
- Large projects in particular should have a *project secretary* assigned to them. With small projects, one of the members of the team could be appointed secretary. The duties of the secretary consist of taking care of the correspondence, taking the minutes of meetings, noting how much time has gone into the tasks (time records) and managing the project's files.
- **Project members** are selected on the basis of their expertise and their capacity to execute the project. They may be recruited from within the organization itself, but may also be brought in from outside. Occasionally the whole of a project is contracted out.
- **Consultants**. These are very often experts from the within organization itself, but consultants from outside may also need to be hired.

Working group
One or more working groups can be established within the project group (see Figure 2.2). The working group is responsible for carrying out a separate sub-task of the project. The working group manager is in charge. When building a new factory, for example, a working group can be put together to organize a festive opening, or, when placing a new product on

the market, a working group might be responsible for the advertising campaign. A working group might even be put together to organize a training course after a totally new information system has been installed at a company.

The outside world

A project group does not do its work in isolation and has a certain relationship with the 'outside world', i.e. the project environment. People from outside the organization may include the following:

- The **sponsor** or client of the project group
- A **steering committee** (see section 2.15)
- A **reference group** or **committee of experts**. This is a group of people experienced in the activities that are required to execute the project. They are available to exchange experiences and act as a sounding board. Few projects have such a committee.
- **Departmental heads**. These individuals provide project members from within the main organization.
- A **representative advisory board** (or other participation committee) that provides advice on the project or is required to give approval for the project.
- The **government**, which provides subsidies and issues permits.

Interaction between the project team and the project environment

While a project group works autonomously, it does have connections with others both inside and outside the parent organization, as is illustrated in Fig. 2.3.

FIGURE 2.3 The project and its environment

There is a certain amount of interplay between people, resources, information and money between the parent organization, the project and the outside world. All interested parties in a project are called "*stakeholders*". Stakeholders can benefit or be harmed by a project and may be able to influence the project. For projects involving large numbers of different stakeholders, a *stakeholder analysis* – also called an *environmental analysis* – is carried out. This analysis provides an overview of all parties involved and their interest in the project. It is used to help determine with whom and how communication should take place. A 'Stakeholder analysis checklist' can be downloaded from the website.

Stakeholders

Stakeholder analysis

External communication is important. The project group needs to let the parent organization and the outside world know what it is doing. This can be done verbally or in writing. The following are some avenues available:

- The company's Intranet site
- The staff magazine
- A special information bulletin
- Announcements on the notice board
- A seminar
- Staff meetings
- Newspaper clippings

External communication

For complicated projects involving large numbers of stakeholders, a *stakeholder analysis* and, if relevant, a special *communication plan*, can be formulated. This plan describes all agreements and activities regarding internal and external communication on the project.

Communication plan

Knowing that others within the organization have been informed about the project can act as a stimulus on the project members.

2.3 Sponsor

The sponsor is the person or organization that requires the product result. This party is the *"client"* of the project group, who wants the project's end product to be put at his disposal and who pays for it, therefore making him the *sponsor* of the project. A project may have more than one sponsor. In this case, it is important for the project manager to designate a contact person, i.e. *one* end client. It is extremely difficult for a project manager if he is forced to deal with more than one client.
The project's schedules provide the sponsor with an indication of when the end product can be expected. He is the one who has the ultimate say in whether the project result is acceptable.

Client

Sponsor

The sponsor instigates the project – possibly on behalf of the board of directors – and has the following responsibilities:

- Making decisions, such as approving a project proposal, approving the project plan, and approving the project result
- Creating clarity in unclear situations
- Making sure there is sufficient authorization from the management board of the organization involved to carry the project through
- Making sure others within the organization see the value of the project, thereby creating sufficient support for the project within the organization
- Having a say in the project group's deliberations
- Monitoring the progress of the project
- Making the funds available and keeping track of them
- Monitoring the quality of the work

If a project does not have a single, clearly identifiable sponsor, the chances that it will be successful are small.

It is often assumed that a sponsor knows exactly what he wants. But this is not always the case in reality. Once the project group starts working and submits the intermediate results, the sponsor may change his mind about certain aspects and demand changes. To ensure the success of the project, the project manager will have to deal with these changes appropriately, such as by having the sponsor or other involved parties submit an official *change request*.

Change request

If a project is successful, the sponsor is often the one to receive the majority of attention (more than the project manager and project group). But if the project is not successful, the sponsor usually accepts his responsibility, but, internally, may blame the project manager. That is why good communication between the sponsor and project manager is so important.

2.4 Future users

As mentioned earlier, a project is started in order to yield a particular project result. This end product is eventually "put into use" by (future) "users". For example, a construction project yields a house in which the new occupants are considered the users of the project result. Patients and nurses are the users of a new hospital wing following its construction, whereas the hospital director is the sponsor. With a project that entails implementing a new computer program, the people who will be working with the new program are the users. Likewise, the users of a project with the goal of organizing a major study trip are the students.

Users

The sponsor pays for the project but it is ultimately the users who must work with its results. It is therefore essential to involve the future users in the project from its onset and to keep them involved throughout the entire project. After all, they can make a professional contribution to achieving the final result. Users are also referred to as "subject experts". It is important that they *accept* the final results of the project. If involved in the project from the very beginning and given the opportunity to get used to the consequences of the project result, there will be a greater chance that the users will accept the results.

Accept

2.5 The project manager

If the project is carried out within a company, the project manager will usually be appointed by the board of directors. Occasionally a project group is allowed to choose a project manager from their midst. If the project is a complicated one, the project manager should be a real "heavyweight". If no one is available to take on the task of being the project manager, an experienced person could be engaged via a consulting agency.

The project manager's task is usually more difficult than that of the other project members, but the very fact that it is challenging can also make it very rewarding. It may be a real learning experience for him or her. It is important to have one – and only one – project manager, because otherwise the sponsor will find it difficult to monitor the project.

This section discusses the competences and responsibilities of a project manager. We will also closely examine the competence of "negotiation skills".

The competences of a project manager

A project manager is sometimes called the "captain of the ship", the "conductor of the orchestra" or the "coach of the team". These colourful descriptions refer to the role played by the project manager. Unlike a line manager, a project manager is the *temporary boss* of his project team. In order to be an effective project manager, he or she requires a good number of competences. A *competence* is a combination of the knowledge, skills, attitude and behaviour needed to be able to function well in a particular professional situation. In other words, a competence is a *professional skill* (Grit, Guit & Van der Sijde, 2004).

Temporary boss

Competence

Professional skill

In choosing a project manager, the right competences ought to be taken into consideration during the selection process. In view of the demands made of a project manager, he or she almost needs to be superhuman. In addition to general management skills, a project manager must be able to work in a systematic and result-oriented fashion. He or she should also be stress-resistant and have a good understanding of company policy.

A project manager should at least possess the following capacities:
- Leadership abilities
- Ability to negotiate, such as with the sponsor
- A task-oriented working style
- Ability to preside over meetings
- Ability to distinguish between main issues and side issues
- Ability to estimate the risks that could threaten the project
- Ability to determine the limits of the project
- Ability to formulate a project plan
- Ability to determine the necessary competences for the project team
- Ability to plan and think ahead
- Ability to monitor quality
- Ability to motivate the members of the project team
- Ability to set up a project organization
- Ability to lead project members
- Ability to organize and delegate
- Ability to manage finances
- Ability to negotiate (with the sponsor and project members, for instance)

Naturally it can be advantageous if the project manager is an *expert in the field* but, depending on the type of project, this is not always necessary - and can even be problematic. Experts may be tempted to focus too much on the details of the project, which might mean that the main lines become less clear. Some large organizations have designated professional project leaders, who work continuously on projects, but are often not an expert in the project subject matter, rather skilled project managers.

Expert in the field

The responsibilities of a project manager
The tasks of a project manager are threefold:
- Management with an internal focus (on the project group)
- Management with an external focus (on the sponsor)
- Organizing

The project manager has a number of responsibilities:
- To make sure there is a good project plan
- To make the project plan known to all participants
- To have the project plan approved by the sponsor
- To report on the progress of the project to the sponsor, especially regarding deployment of people and funds
- To take care of the external communication, including consulting with

and reporting to the sponsor and the departmental heads that have provided the project with its manpower
- To request or even demand clarification by the sponsor in respect of any unclear situations
- To take on the day-to-day leadership of the team
- To preside over the project team meetings
- To keep the project team enthusiastic
- To resolve any problems that might arise between team members or between team members and others within the organization
- To stand up for and protect his team members during conflicts with people outside the project
- To delegate the work within the team
- To plan aspects of the project along with the team members
- To monitor whether things are being done within the allocated time frames
- To monitor the project's budget
- To monitor the quality of the products produced
- To prescribe the tools and techniques to be used by the team, including the chart techniques and the computer software to be used.

Program manager
Project manager

Sometimes a distinction is made between a project manager and a *program manager*. A *project manager* is responsible for one project only, whereas a program manager may be in charge of several projects, each with their own project leader.

2.6 The project members

Sponsors

The *project members* and the *project manager* – together the *sponsors* - carry out the project. They are often selected based on their individual competences. Employees who perform well within the company are usually chosen to serve on a project team. A project manager must find the right members for the project team together with the sponsor. After all, the quality of the project members is essential for the success of the project.

The project members should possess a variety of competences:
- They should be able to agree on a division of tasks between them and plan the activities efficiently.
- They should encourage a creative atmosphere, so that all good ideas get heard.
- They should give each team member the opportunity to take the initiative within the framework of the project.
- They should be able to hold effective discussions.
- They should be able to deal with differences of opinion and conflicts within the team.
- They should be able to reach agreement on decisions.
- They should be able to give and accept criticism.

Project members have the following responsibilities:
- To execute the tasks that have been set in consultation with the project manager in a correct and efficient manner
- To meet their deadlines as laid down in consultation with the project manager

- To report to the project manager on the results obtained as well as on the time spent (time records)
- To keep the managers of the department where they normally work informed

2.7 Task-oriented and people-oriented leadership

A project team is made up of a number of people who have come together to perform a task. If a project manager is solely *task-oriented* or solely people-oriented the project will suffer. A task-oriented project manager who wants to impress the sponsor will try to get a large project done in as short a time as he possibly can. He will not realize that he is setting his project workers an almost impossible task and they might get into difficulty. On the other hand, if a *people-oriented* project manager constantly tries to please his workers, the job will suffer.

Task-oriented

People-oriented

A project manager who is neither task-oriented nor people-oriented is known as a *deserter*: somebody who shirks his responsibilities. Such a manager pays little attention to his team and the result is that interaction between the group members determines what is done. This approach makes the members uncertain about what is expected of them and leaves them without a clear direction. This type of leadership is called *laisser faire* (literally: letting go) leadership and is really not leadership at all. Exactly the opposite approach is authoritarian leadership. Most employees hate *authoritarian leadership*, but they also hate it when a leader ignores his responsibilities. Management can also be regarded as a service to the employees: the manager takes care of a lot of things for the employees so that they can get on with their work in peace.

Deserter

Laisser faire

Authoritarian leadership

2.8 Working on a project

The success of a project depends largely on the ability of the project team to work together as a whole. *Teambuilding* is therefore of the utmost importance. Teambuilding involves getting a group of individuals together and getting them to collaborate together as a unit. Training can be an instrument in achieving this. See Figure 2.4.

Teambuilding

FIGURE 2.4 Teambuilding: everyone rowing in the same direction

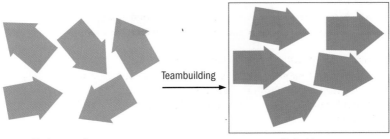

Project members   Project team

Division of roles

While some of the project members will probably have worked on a project before, for others it might be the first time. In order for a project to be successful, each and every member of the team must know what can be expected of the other members. There should be clear agreement about the *division of roles* – including those of the project manager, secretary and filing secretary – and they should be divided on the basis of aptitude and experience.

Project plan
Consultants

The tasks of the various team members are laid down before the commencement of the project in a *project plan*. *Consultants* are sometimes hired in to take part in the project. These are likely to be external advisers working part-time on a project in their capacity as experts. They usually have the advantage of being flexible because they have been used to changes, and sometimes have a great deal of experience. Moreover, they can operate more freely within the organization because they do not have to make their careers in the organization they are detached to.

Job hoppers

Some employees like working in a project-based manner and work on them as often as they can. They are known as *job hoppers*, because they move from project to project or even from job to job. If they leave a project before it is finished it can have a detrimental effect on the results.

Stress

Working on a project can cause *stress*. Not everybody is able to work under pressure for long periods of time. After a long project, it is advisable to allocate employees who are susceptible to stress less demanding tasks.

Career conflict
Two-boss
problem

Project workers are usually recruited via the departmental heads of the organization. Such a project member has, in fact, two bosses: the project manager and the head of his own department. For the advancement of his career he is dependent on the head of his department, who advises on promotion and salary increases. A project member may therefore be tempted to heed his departmental head rather than the project manager. This is known as *career conflict* or the "*two-boss problem*" (see Figure 2.5).

FIGURE 2.5 Who is my boss?

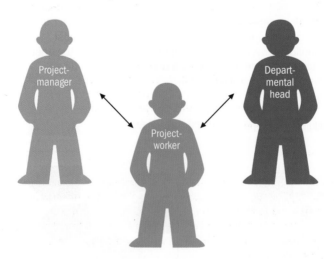

When a departmental head lends out one of his employees to work on a project, he probably will have to do the same amount of work in his department with less manpower. He is therefore likely to be unhappy about losing that employee. The project manager should be aware of the conflicts that might arise from this, and should try to keep a good relationship with both the head of the department and with the project member himself.

2.9 Team roles according to Belbin

Some project teams function perfectly while others perform less efficiently or poorly. Organizational expert *Belbin* (Belbin, 1999) has conducted extensive research into this topic. He has identified nine roles that people play in a team (including project teams). The following is a brief description of these various roles.

Belbin

1 Implementer
Motto: "Stop complaining and get to work"
The implementer (male or female) is a hard worker with good common sense, considerable self-discipline and practical. He or she is a good -organizer, systematic and task-oriented. This go-getter is less flexible and does not often come up with new ideas, nor is he or she always open to new ideas.

2 Co-ordinator
Motto: "Let's not stray from the topic"
The co-ordinator knows how to command respect, is often domineering and knows how to make the most of other people's abilities. He or she is good at motivating and delegating and is goal-oriented, calm and self-confident. He or she is not always exceptionally creative or intelligent.

3 Shaper
Motto: "We need to get out of it what we can"
The shaper has a lot of energy, is driven, ambitious, extraverted and dynamic. He or she combines ideas and points out priorities and goals. He or she is often impatient, insistent and irritable.

4 Plant
Motto: "This is an interesting problem, a real challenge"
The plant is an imaginative individualist with a lot of original ideas. He or she is intelligent, individualistic and can play an important role during brainstorming sessions. He or she has a tendency to disregard practical details, is often careless and is sensitive to criticism.

5 Resource investigator
Motto: "I'll look into it; I know some people"
The resource investigator is curious, enthusiastic, communicative, extraverted and has a capacity for contacting people. He or she is a real "networker" and brings in new ideas from the outside world. This person can sometimes be too optimistic, bores easily and has a tendency to fail to meet commitments, but is often good at improvising. He or she can be domineering and overenthusiastic.

6   Monitor evaluator

Motto: "Let's give it a good thought and explore all the possibilities first"
The monitor evaluator has a sound sense of judgment, is competent, critical, unemotional, professional and cautious. He or she often has little inspiration, is not very enthusiastic and afraid to make decisions too quickly. He or she can be rude and tactless.

7   Team worker

Motto: "Let's keep things positive; everyone has their own strengths"
The team worker is people-oriented, diplomatic, promotes team spirit, is sensitive and responds positively to others. Like a coach, he or she stimulates strong team members and helps less strong team members. He or she tries to avoid problems and is often passive. The team worker often has difficultly making hard decisions.

8   Completer finisher

Motto: "Only the best is good enough"
The completer is orderly, quality conscious, a perfectionist and conscientious, but often tense. He or she is well able to finish things and encourages and controls other. However, this person has a hard time delegating and is sometimes too concerned about the details.

9   Specialist

Motto: "That's not my area of experience; I don't know much about that"
The specialist possesses considerable professional knowledge and tries to expand on this. He or she goes it alone and often gets stuck in the technical details, has little feel for the big picture and does not get involved in matters outside of his or her area of expertise.

10   Mix

Of the nine roles described by Belbin, one person can fulfil a combination of roles, such as the company man and completer, at the same time.

Belbin test

Belbin's research has shown that a productive team combines a variety of different roles. In a team with mostly company men, a lot of work gets done but very few creative solutions are found, whereas a team with primarily shapers comes up with a lot of creative ideas, but little gets done. The Belbin test is therefore a good method for putting together a well-balanced team in which there is a good mix of team roles. The need for various team roles may also depend on the team's task and whether or not any restrictions have been placed on the team composition.

Belbin developed various tests for determining what kind of role or roles people play in a team. These tests are included in his book, although they can also be found and taken online. Once completed, they give a good impression of which team role(s) a person plays.

2.10 Virtual tools for collaboration

Computers, business networks and the Internet have made it possible to work together in a (project) group in a different and more efficient manner. The following are a few examples of virtual tools.

Agenda management

It can often be difficult to make agreements with project members or others involved in the project. An *electronic agenda* can be extremely helpful in this regard. This agenda allows you to send an invitation by e-mail to other meeting participants or compare your agenda with another person's agenda directly when scheduling a meeting. Examples of agendas are MS Outlook for computer use and Google Agenda on the Internet. Both of these can be used with your mobile phone, which automatically updates your agreements and e-mail.

Electronic agenda

Teleconferencing

Ensuring that a project runs smoothly requires considerable collaboration. That is why the project team, steering committee and other involved parties must meet often. Meetings not only require considerable time, but also money, especially if the participants have to travel to the meeting from other parts of the country, thereby incurring travel expenses and – even more costly – travelling time. That is why more and more organisations use teleconferencing services. This makes it possible for more than two people to talk and runs through a phone line, radio link or the Internet. If they are also able to see one another, this is called *videoconferencing*. There are several providers that offer this service, such as phone companies and specialised companies. After you have agreed on a time, you both call in at the same time or are called by the organiser of the 'conference'. The Skype program also allows you to video chat online free of charge with one or more persons at the same time (but without seeing each other).

Videoconferencing

Sharing documents

While a project is being carried out, numerous documents are often produced, such as project proposals, the project plan, minutes, reports, calculations and presentations. Naturally you want these documents to be easily available to certain individuals involved in the project. One option is to place the files on the company Intranet site, although, in this case, they will not often available outside the company for you or other project members who do not work at the company. You could also consider placing the files on a document-sharing website. One such website, *Google Documents* allows you to edit documents online using your browser. The files are stored on the Google servers and you can grant access to others to read and/or revise them. With *Microsoft Office Live*, you can use MS Word or another word processor – and all the options it comes with – to share and revise your texts. In this case, you can use the 'track changes' function so that other users can see exactly what changes you have made to the document.

Google Documents

Microsoft Office Live

Planning software

Planning software allows you to schedule all of the activities of project members and tools, thereby informing all project members exactly when which action is expected of them. This software also allows you to easily create Gantt charts (see Chapter 4), draw up a list of tasks, carry out financial calculations, keep track of progress, conduct what-if analysis and so on. This type of software is indispensable for large projects with numerous activities and resources. Examples include MS Project and Open Workbench (free). These programs can be installed on a personal computer or local computer network. Other planning programs do not have to be

**Time
registration**

installed but are available online. These programs often require that you pay an annual subscription fee for every participant. It is also sometimes possible to have project members record their hours spend using this software, i.e. for.

Virtual collaboration

You can collaborate on your organisation's local network or you could also take advantage of providers that allow you to log onto a website to access a wide range of collaboration tools. Some of the functions these offer are sharing common files, revising documents online, e-mailing groups, holding discussions, exchanging ideas, sharing knowledge, drawing up schedules, monitoring schedules, time registration, budget monitoring and creating and monitoring lists of action points.

Social networking

Social networks allow you to connect and maintain social contacts with people who may be of help to you at some point. Examples are the ever-popular Facebook and the more serious LinkedIn, aimed at profession- als. With LinkedIn, you share contact persons – called connections – and can share information with each other through Groups. LinkedIn also makes it possible to locate hard-to-find experts for your project.

2.11 **Team agreements**

In order to ensure that a project team can work together effectively and efficiently, it is advisable to first make a number of clear *team agreements* during the first project meeting (see Chapter 6). The agreements made are then included in the meeting report (minutes). If someone fails to stand by the agreements, he or she can be held accountable for this.

**Team
agreements**

The following are a number of examples of team agreements on coopera- tion that can be made within a project group:
1   Everyone accepts the project assignment.
2   Everyone is equally responsible for the outcome.
3   Every team member is given the opportunity to contribute.
4   We respect each other and listen to the opinions of others.
5   We communicate openly and provide honest feedback in case of conflict.
6   No complaining allowed.
7   We do not promise anything we cannot deliver.
8   We stick to the agreements made.
9   If someone fails to stick to the agreements made, we hold him or her accountable for this.
10   The decision-making process is determined beforehand (see section 2.13).
11   Everyone must attend the project meetings. If you are unable to attend, you must notify the chairperson.
12   The project manager is the only person in direct contact with the sponsor.
13   The project manager presides over the meetings.
14   The role of minute secretary is performed in turns according to a set schedule.

15   Meeting reports (minutes) must be submitted within three days or there is not point to having action items.
16   Time is set aside at the start of every meeting for "catching up".
17   Meetings start on time and do not go over time.
18   No making calls or accepting calls during meetings. All cell phones must be switched off.
19   A brief evaluation is made at the end of every meeting.

Agreements are also made on the use of the 'Virtual tools for collaboration' from section 2.10. You can choose a number of these agreements and tools and change them as needed.

The International Project Management Association (IPMA) is an association of professionals specialising in project management. They have formulated a *code of conduct* for the ethical aspects of project collaboration. This code of conduct is aimed at ensuring a professional execution of projects by its members. It refers to ethical matters such as respect, trust, meticulousness, sufficient communication, constructive actions, independence, socially responsible practices, loyalty to the sponsor, expertise, responsibilities, legal issues, honesty, influence and acceptance payment. The entire code can be found online by Googling 'IPMA, code of conduct, wiki'.

Code of conduct

2.12 Brainstorming

An essential aspect of a project is that it involves solving a previously unsolved problem or performing a new task. This requires creativity on the part of the project members. This can be stimulated by brainstorming sessions. During a *brainstorming session* – a session is a meeting – a group of ideas are expressed freely. The goal is to come up with as many different solutions as possible, with every participant being given plenty of opportunity to contribute. Brainstorming sessions are most effective when lead by someone with experience. He or she introduces the topic, is in charge of the session and makes sure the rules are followed. He or she can also write down the ideas and solutions suggested on a whiteboard or make them visible to the participants in some other way.

Brainstorming session

To ensure an effective brainstorming session, the following *brainstorming rules* apply:
- There are no good, bad or strange ideas during a brainstorming session. Whether or not an idea is feasible is not important. The goal is to come up with as many ideas as possible. Once the brainstorming session has ended, all ideas can be examined for their feasibility.
- During the brainstorming session, no one may criticize the ideas of others. This is only allowed at the end of the session after everyone has contributed ideas.
- It is permitted to combine or add one's own ideas to the ideas of others.

Brainstorming rules

To get the most out of a brainstorming session, participants should be informed about the subject beforehand. Before starting with the actual issue at hand, a more casual topic can be chosen first to brainstorm about in order to get everyone in the right mood and stimulate their creative impulses.

In addition to brainstorming, there are other methods for stimulating creativity in a group of people, such as the Delphi method, the nominal method and mind mapping (Grit & Gerritsma, 2006).

2.13 Negotiating

Negotiating

One of the things a project manager needs to be very good at is *negotiating*. Negotiation involves two parties with more or less opposing interests trying to defend their own interests as much as possible.

The project manager may have to negotiate in a variety of situations:
- With the sponsor concerning the project's budget, the project's schedules and the scope of the project (what the project covers and what it does not)
- With suppliers concerning prices and delivery times
- With project members concerning the quality of their work and when it has to be done by
- With department heads concerning staffing the project
- With government bodies concerning permits and subsidies

There are many good handbooks and courses on negotiating, so there is no need to deal with it here in any detail, but we have put together a number of tips:
- Be well prepared and well-informed on the subject.
- Determine beforehand what the goal is and what the extent of your bargaining margin is.
- Work out your strategy beforehand. You might decide to listen to what the other party has to offer before making an offer.
- Try to avoid personal animosities and concentrate entirely on the desired result.
- Show respect for your opponent, because both parties in a negotiation situation are served by a favourable outcome.
- Show some understanding of your opponent's position.
- Do not reproach or blame the other party and try and avoid conflicts and quarrels.
- Do not allow yourself to be put under pressure. If an agreement is not forthcoming it might be better to break off negotiations and continue them at a later date or to call for independent arbitration.
- If you think you have come out on top in the negotiations, gloating is to be avoided. A good negotiator is always respectful of the opponent. Quite possibly they might have to do business again in the future.

2.14 Making decisions in a project

Project managers, project members and sponsors are all required to make decisions. During project meetings, for example, decisions must be made regarding suitable solutions for problems.

There are several different ways that decisions can be made within a group (Schein, 2001). A project manager can choose the most appropriate decision-making process for the situation.

Decision-making based on majority vote

After the discussion, the proposal desired by the majority of participants is accepted. The down side to this method is that those who did not vote in favour of the proposal might feel that they have "lost" and this can become problematic when carrying out the decision.

Decision-making based on consensus

With decision-making based on consensus, the group continues discussing the issue until everyone is able to live with the decision. Everyone gets the opportunity to make comments. No vote is held, so the members of the group who are less enthusiastic do not feel that they have "lost". This decision-making method can be time-consuming but is highly effective.

Decision-making based on unanimity

With decision-making based on unanimity, everyone is unanimous about the proposal. In other words, no one has any objections to it.

Decision-making as a result of a lack of response

In this case, proposals are made continuously until one is made that receives a positive response. The earlier proposals are then silently rejected.

Decision-making based on authority

A project manager has the formal authority in the project since he or she is the "boss". Because of this authority, he or she can make the final decision at the end of the discussion. Since the sponsor is the one funding the project, he or she is in turn the project manager's "boss". Authority can also be the result of expertise in a particular subject area, on which the decision is then based.

Decision-making based on automatic approval

If a decision must be made suddenly within a group, some members might feel caught off guard, since they have not had the time to explore the problem, and therefore do not respond. When the chairperson asks, "Does anyone object?" they do not respond and the proposal is then approved. This decision-making method can result in a decision that is made by the minority. If the chairperson had asked, "Who is in favour of this proposal?" the decision might have turned out differently.

2.15 Related projects

The goal of a project is to yield a concrete result in a short period of time. The desired results, however, are sometimes so extensive or complicated that several different projects are carried out alongside one another in order to achieve the ultimate goal.

Steering committees are often established when several related projects take place simultaneously. A *steering committee* (see Figure 2.6) consists of the sponsor's representative – such as a member of the board of directors – and the project managers of the various projects. The steering committee is responsible for the exchange of information and coordination between the different projects. They also monitor the progress of the

Steering committee

projects and make sure there is sufficient support within the organization. The steering committee advises the sponsor.

FIGURE 2.6 Projects with a steering committee

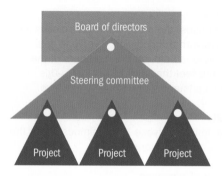

○ = Linking pin

Linking pin

Figure 2.6 shows the principle of the *"linking pin"*. The leader of the group is also a member of a "higher" group and connects (links) both groups. The people who serve as the linking pins make sure that the necessary information gets exchanged. The principle of the linking pin was explained in relation to working groups in Figure 2.2.

Program
Organization's
goals

A number of related projects are sometimes called a *"program"*. The goal of a program is to achieve the *organization's goals*. It requires not only projects, but also activities in the line organization. Programs are found in all kinds of large organizations, including government agencies, power companies, multinationals and oil companies. Examples of programs are the construction of a residential neighbourhood, a merger between two companies, the installation of comprehensive business software or the construction of a new factory, hospital or oil platform. If a company aims to carry out a program like "establishing a new factory", this could include projects like "constructing a factory building", "hiring suitable personnel", "setting up a production line", "automation activities" and "establishing a power supply". In addition to these individual projects, the line organization staff would also be involved in the program. See Figure 2.7.

Task force

If a project group consists of a group of employees who have been chosen as a group to carry out a large project, this is called a *"task force"*. This group is often housed in a separate area in order to enable them to concentrate their efforts on the task at hand.

FIGURE 2.7 Program management and project management

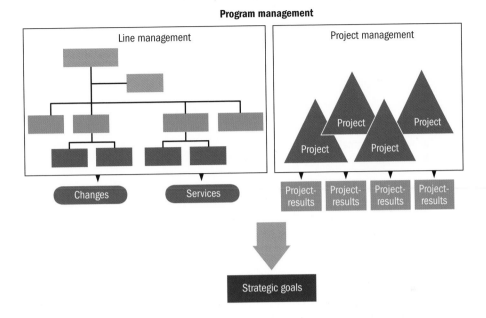

2.16 Outsourcing a project

External firms may provide the staff for a project. Staff agencies very often   **Staff agencies**
have people capable of various specialized tasks on their books, including
project managers, designers and financial experts. Computer experts are
also very frequently hired through *employment agencies*.

Some projects are completely contracted out to external service companies. This is frequently the case with computer projects. Contracting out
those tasks that are not part of the *core business* of a company is known   **Core business**
as "*outsourcing*". This involves the independent execution of certain   **Outsourcing**
activities by an external company, with fixed agreements about the required
results, very often for a *fixed price* and to be ready on a *fixed date*.   **Fixed price**
A project that complies completely with these prerequisites and which is   **Fixed date**
contracted out entirely is called a *turnkey project*. The sponsor receives the   **Turnkey project**
required product against a set price at a set time. All he has to do is to
"turn the key" to use what the project has produced. Computer systems
and projects in the areas of house building, shipbuilding and technology are
very often turnkey projects.

Before a turnkey project is carried out, the supplier makes an *offer* to the
sponsor, i.e. the client, which contains a price for providing the project
results. The website explains how to put together a project offer.

Assignments

2.1 Drawn an organizational chart for:
a A bread factory
b An organization that you know of

2.2 What does "A project organization is separate from the normal line organization" mean?

2.3 "A project should have one (and only one) sponsor. A project manager should not accept the job if the situation is otherwise". Comment.

2.4 Section 1.2 gives examples of projects. Choose ten projects (alone or together with your instructor) and indicate who the users of the project results would be.

2.5 List two reasons why the users of a project's end result should be involved in the project process.

2.6 Indicate whether the project manager's responsibilities as described in this chapter are internal, external or organizational.

2.7 a What does "A project manager should have insight into company policy" mean?
b "A project manager should be an expert in the subject of the project". Comment.

2.8 Suggest two reasons why a project manager should pay attention to good information and public relations.

2.9 What communicative skills are needed to work on a project? Which of these do you yourself possess? Which do you lack, and how can you go about acquiring them?

2.10 A seminar is being arranged at some holiday resort to make sure that "everyone is rowing in the same direction". What might be the point of this seminar?

2.11 What two advantages does hiring in consultants have? Can you think of a disadvantage?

2.12 Discuss in groups what measures a project manager can take to ensure that the project group works effectively and efficiently.

2.13   What is meant by the following:
  a An organizational chart
  b A line organization
  c A competence
  d A steering committee
  e A committee of experts
  f A working group
  g A subject expert
  h A stakeholder
  i Laisser faire (with regard to leadership)
  j Task-oriented leadership
  k People-oriented leadership
  l Authoritarian leadership
  m Teambuilding
  n A consultant
  o A job hopper
  p Career conflict
  q Brainstorming
  r Employment agency
  s Core business
  t Outsourcing
  u Fixed price project
  v Fixed date project
  w A turnkey project

2.14 **a** Explain why determining which Belbin team role(s) a person plays can benefit a project.
  b Which Belbin team roles are absolutely necessary in order to put together a good project team? Which project tasks are they needed for?
  c Re-examine the team roles in section 2.9. Which two roles suit you best?
  d Carrying out the Belbin test:
   • Find a Belbin test online and take it.
   • Which team roles apply to you?
   • How well do these roles match the ones you listed for point c of this assignment?
   • Compare "your" roles with those of your team mates. Is there enough variety in the team?
  e The resource investigator is a "networker". What does this mean exactly?

2.15   List one advantage and one disadvantage of contracting out a project as a turnkey project.

2.16   When a large reorganization involves involuntary dismissals, some companies hire a temporary project manager from outside the company. Explain why this is preferable to bringing in a project manager from within the company.

2.17   Which of the decision-making processes discussed in section 2.14 is used by your project group? Give examples.

2.18   Organize a brainstorming session in accordance with the guidelines of section 2.12 with the following topics:
   a Organizing an outing for your department
   b A new project
   c A topic of your choice

2.19 a What is the difference between a "project" and a "program"?
   b What is a steering committee?
   c What is a task force?

2.20   Discuss the following statements in groups:
   a Being a project manager is a full-time job.
   b Not everybody can learn to be a project manager.
   c A project manager should be familiar with all the details of his project.
   d Everybody is capable of working on a project.
   e A project manager should be more task-oriented than people-oriented.
   f A vaguely formulated project goal could be to the advantage of the project's sponsor.
   g By letting people work on a project you enable them to become experts in the field.

3
The project from start to finish

A project's life cycle consists of three stages: preliminary organization, execution and completion. To ensure the desired result, it is important that all three stages receive full attention from both the sponsor and project team.

This chapter therefore covers such topics as writing a project proposal, the initial meeting between the project manager and sponsor, and setting up and carrying out a project.

3.1 Organizing and carrying out the project

If the organization has little or no experience in working on projects, it is recommended that it do a small *trial project* first. This will enable everybody to get used to the work approach a project requires, and should the trial project fail, the loss to the company will be minimal. A trial project is also known as a *pilot project*.

Larger projects are carried out in phases. Section 1.7 introduced the various phases of a project: concept, definition, preliminary design, detailed design, production and aftercare. Aftercare is necessary once the project results have been achieved by the project group and are used and maintained (often by others). This chapter covers the entire process from concept to the delivery of the project results, which is shown schematically from concept to the official conclusion of the project in Figure 3.1.

FIGURE 3.1 Global outline of a project

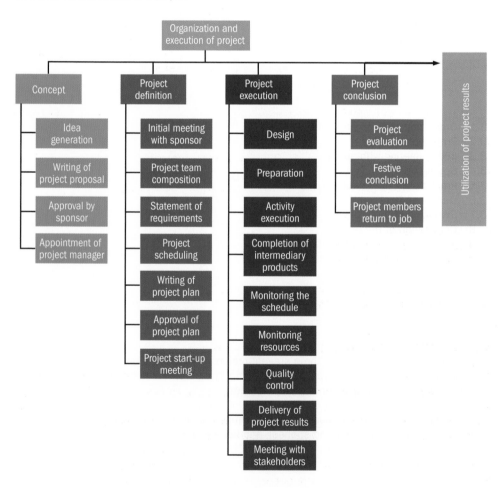

Figure 3.1 provides a detailed overview of the phases shown in Figure 1.3 in Chapter 1. The utilization of the project results and aftercare are not discussed in detail in this book because they fall outside the responsibility of the project group. After all, once the project is completed, the project results are transferred to the sponsor and users.

Some of the more important elements from Figure 3.1 are explained in subsequent sections (3.2 to 3.8),. A detailed explanation of how to write a project plan is provided in a separate chapter (Chapter 5).

3.2 Project proposal

Starting up a new project can be a major undertaking. People from not only the organization itself but also often from outside the organization need to work together to get the project done. The execution of the project can involve high costs. Since the project might result in a change to how people carry out their work, the start-up phase of a project can be a touchy subject "politically", i.e. there could be some resistance to the project.
Whether or not a project is started up is therefore a decision that needs to be made by management. To prepare for this, the *idea* for the project is often outlined in a project proposal during the *concept phase* (also see section 1.7). This proposal can be written up at the initiative of an employee or at the request of management.

Idea
Concept phase

Important aspects of a project proposal are:
- Name of the project
- Introduction and background to the project
- Information on the person who has written the project proposal
- Future sponsor
- As detailed description as possible of the project results; scheduling outline
- People and resources required
- Cost estimate
- Feasibility and expected bottlenecks
- Consequences for the organization

Once the project proposal is approved, management usually appoints a project manager to further develop the proposal.

3.3 Initial meeting with the sponsor

Projects are often based on a rather vague idea. It takes someone with enough influence and budget (money) in the organization to carry out this idea in the form of a project. Since this person is the sponsor, he chooses a project manager to lead the project team. The sponsor invites the project leader to talk about the matter. This conversation is called the "*initial meeting*". During this meeting, the outline of the project is determined by means of brainstorming and discussion. A good project manager tries to acquire as clear a picture as possible of the ultimate results of the project, the amount of money available, which persons are available, what should be included in the project and when it should be completed. The project

Initial meeting

Negotiate

manager will not immediately be able or willing to say "yes" or "no" to every aspect, but usually requests some time to think about it first. He will often have to *negotiate* with the sponsor about such matters as more money and more available project members (see section 2.13 on negotiating). The project is defined in more detail during subsequent meetings between these parties.

3.4 Setting up the project

Feasibility study

Go/no-go decision

If there is some ambivalence about the project, a *feasibility study* could be carried out first. A definite decision on whether or not to embark on the project would be made subject to the findings of the feasibility study: the *go/no-go decision*. If a decision to go ahead is made, a number of things have to be organized:
- The objectives of the project must be determined.
- A team has to be put together and suitable people for that team have to be found. Permission for them to be on the team must be obtained. Some thought also has to be given to how the tasks should be divided.
- Authorization to make decisions must be arranged. What decisions should be made by the project group itself? What decisions should be authorized beforehand and by whom?
- Lines of communication have to be organized. The management board and the members of the team have to be kept informed of the progress of the project.

Project plan

All this should be put down in writing during the definition phase of the project (see section 1.7) and a *project plan* drawn up. Making a good project plan is of the utmost importance for the success of a project. The drawing up of a good project plan will be treated in detail in Chapter 5.

3.5 Project start-up meeting

Start-up
Kick-off

Projects get underway officially during a *start-up meeting* at which all the stakeholders and participants – sponsor, project members and so on – should be present. The start-up meeting is sometimes known as the "*kick-off*" meeting (the project "kicks off" at this point).

The start-up meeting should foster a feeling of solidarity among those involved in the project. Ideally, the meeting should be held in pleasant surroundings away from the everyday working environment. Organizing meetings will be dealt with in Chapter 6. A start-up meeting could have the following agenda items:
- **Getting acquainted** with each other: finding out who everybody is, what areas they are specialized in and what everybody expects from the project. Those present could be asked to introduce themselves or activities could be organized to allow the members of the team to get to know each other better (teambuilding).
- Discussion of the **goals** of the project. This could be useful for finding out whether all people involved have the same ideas about the goals of the project.
- Presentation of the **project plan**. Instructions on how to give a presentation are given in Chapter 10.

- Discussion of the **activities** to be carried out, the deadline for each activity and who will carry them out.
- The methods and tools to be used during the project could be explained at this stage.
- **Agreement** has to be reached on the methods and procedures to be followed, including the chart techniques and computer software to be used, how reports should be made and how the time spent should be recorded.
- Team agreements need to be made about what the project members can expect from one another and how they will be collaborating, i.e. a code of conduct. Section 2.10 gives several examples of such agreements.
- The **authority** the group has needs to be made clear. What decisions can the group itself make, and for what decisions does the sponsor have to be consulted first?

If the members are not used to working on projects, a preliminary course in project management could be held.

3.6 Design and preparation

Once the project has gotten underway, a *design* of the project results is usually drawn up (see section 1.7). This design contains a detailed description of the project results to be achieved, i.e. the final outcome. The design is based on the requirements established in the project plan. The design is a document intended for:

Design
Detailed description of the project results

- The sponsor of the project and the users of the project results. The design must make clear to them what they can expect at the end of the project.
- The members of the project team. The design must contain enough information to be able to prepare and carry out the project in order to achieve the project results.

The design is used to make preparations for the project. Once this has been worked out on paper, it is called a detailed design. This contains all the *details* of the project execution. In other words, it is a kind of road map for achieving the project results. In some projects the preliminary and detailed designs coincide, resulting in a single design that answers all the "how's" and "what's".

Detailed design

How

3.7 Execution of the project

After the project has commenced, the project will be carried out based on the specifications of the project plan. The progress that the project is making should be evaluated periodically and the *schedule* adjusted if necessary (also see also Chapter 4 on planning and scheduling). A project that is not managed well can get out of hand, with high costs, delays or even unintended project outcomes. If the project is a large one, this could even jeopardize the company. Projects require *considerable monitoring*. This is dealt with in detail in sections 3.9 and 3.10.

Schedule

Considerable monitoring

3.8 Completion of the project

A project should not only get underway properly (a project plan and a project start-up meeting), it should also be concluded properly. All parties involved need to be informed that the project has been completed. The following points should be kept in mind:

- Depending on the type of project, a final report should be produced.
- After the project has been completed its members will return to their former positions. If the organization has not prepared for this well in advance, this could present difficulties since the project member's original position may have been taken over by another staff member who is doing a good job.
- For some team members, completion of the project can be quite an emotional experience.
- The project manager should make sure that the sponsor provides an official written discharge from the project.
- The project should be officially concluded during a meeting with the sponsor, the project members and the other parties involved.
- At this meeting the outcomes of the project could be presented (see Chapter 10 on presentations)
- **Evaluation** The project results should be *evaluated*. The purpose of this is to avoid repeating any mistakes that have been made in future projects. A *comparison between the predicted costs and actual costs* is an important aspect of evaluation.
- It is a good idea for there to be a dinner party or something similar prior to or after the final meeting.

Comparison between predicted and actual costs

3.9 Monitoring aspects of a project

When buying something – a car for example – there are three important questions that must be asked:

1. What am I getting and what quality? If buying a car, this could be the make and model, year of construction, technical specifications, accessories and the technical condition of the car.
2. When will I get it? A car usually has a delivery period of several days to several months.
3. What will it cost? This depends on the car model and make, as well as any additional accessories and technical specifications.

The same three questions can be asked by the sponsor of a project. He or she has commissioned the project and wants to know what kind of quality can be expected upon completion, when it will be finished and what it will cost. The problem is that every project is unique and usually quite complicated. As a result, the final completion date and costs of the desired results are far less certain than when buying a car. A sponsor is buying something that will not be finished until a future date. So, to prevent the project from failing, it must be monitored closely.

Five monitoring aspects

The following *five monitoring aspects* are therefore essential during the preparation and execution of a project:

1. Time   T
2. Money   M

3 Quality   Q
4 Information   I
5 Organization   O

The project manager and sponsor must pay the right amount of attention to
each of these *TMQIO* factors to ensure a successful project. For example,   **TMQIO**
the project manager has to make sure that the project sticks closely to its
time schedule throughout the preparation and execution of the project.   **Time**
He or she should also know at every stage how much of the *money* has   **Money**
been spent and how much is left. The money made available for the project
is referred to as the "*budget*". The project members have to do their jobs   **Budget**
properly for the outcomes of the interim products and final results to be of
the desired *quality*. The right information is essential for ensuring every-   **Quality**
body knows what he has to do. The sponsor should also be *informed* about   **Information**
the project's progress. The project manager is responsible for the *organiza-*   **Organization**
tion of the project. This includes matters such as internal and external
collaboration, decision making, delegating responsibility and organizing
meetings. The monitoring aspects of a project are shown schematically in
Figure 3.2.

FIGURE 3.2 Monitoring aspects TMQIO of a project

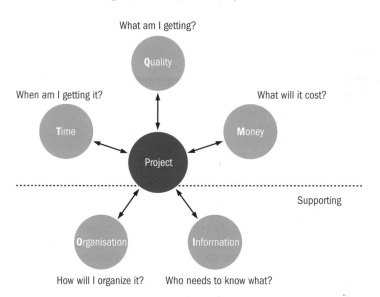

As stated above, the sponsor wants to know what he is getting and what
quality (Q), when he is getting it (T) and what it will cost (M). The monitoring
aspects of organization (O) and information (I) are not a goal in themselves
but rather serve to support the other three aspects.

3.10 Monitoring projects in practice

There are a number of practical matters that have to be attended to during a project. The letters TMQIO indicate the monitoring aspects that these matters fall under and are described in this section.

Pre-planning (T)

Schedule
To ensure the success of a project, a *schedule* must be made beforehand. A number of questions must be answered in drawing up this schedule:
- Which activities must be carried out and how many working hours (time spent) are required for each activity? It is often necessary to consult an export in answering these questions.
- What is the sequence (dependence) of the activities? In other words, what must be done before an activity can be started?
- What **resources** are needed? Resources are the people who will be carrying out the activities plus the tools necessary to do so.
- At what point in time must or can the activity be finished? This pertains to the turnaround time, i.e. the time that elapses between the start and end of an activity.

Chapter 4 discusses scheduling in detail. A good planning tool that can be used for scheduling is the MS Project program. The "Mini-course on MS Project" can be downloaded as a PDF file from the website accompanying this book.

Progress checks (T and I)

Clear arrangements must be made on how project members are to account for their use of time and materials to the project manager.

Time record
Time recording is one way of doing this. A *time record* is a register of each activity in the project plan. It shows the following:
- A description of the activity
- The time spent on it
- The time still needed
- The time originally planned
- The reason for deviating from the original schedules

Forms for the purpose of time recording could be made available (an example can be found on the website accompanying this book). Software especially for time recording is also available. It has the advantage that each team member can register the hours that he works on an activity on his own computer. The project manager can view these records centrally per activity and per project.

Weekly report
A project member can also be asked to write a short weekly report in which the activities that have been carried out during the past week and the activities planned for the next week are set out.

Consulting (I and O)

In order to exchange information, consultations must be held continuously between all parties involved in the project. Project meetings in particular are essential and often take the form of a weekly progress meeting. During this meeting, the project members discuss the progress of the report, update one another and agree on action points. The project manager and sponsor also often stay in contact in order to update each other on the progress being made by means of biweekly meetings. In addition to these more formal meetings at scheduled intervals, informal consultations also take place throughout the entire project between the parties involved by means of e-mail, phone calls and informal office visits.

Adjusting the schedules (T)

Project schedules rarely correspond to reality and the project manager will usually find that they have to be adjusted in the light of the actual situation. If major adjustments are required, the project manager will have to report them to the sponsor and consult with him. A more detailed explanation of schedules can be found in Chapter 4.

Sticking to the project's budget (G)

Before the project is initiated, the size of the budget (amount available) must be determined. The sponsor is the one who makes this *budget*   **Budget**
available. In other words, he "buys" the final results of the project, the "*end*   **End product**
product". The amount of funding available is often determined by means of negotiation between the project manager and sponsor. The budget is used for the people working on the project and the resources required.
How much of the project's budget has been spent and what the *costs* to   **Costs**
date have been must be known at every point of the project. Comparing them with the project's progress will show whether the project is likely to stay within the original budget or turn out to be more expensive.
It is also a good idea to regularly check whether the original estimation of *benefits* or profits is still valid. If during the course of the project it appears   **Benefits**
that the profits are likely to be dramatically less than originally planned, the sponsor may consider adjusting the project's objectives or even terminate the project.

Quality control (K)

A product is of acceptable quality if it contains the properties (specifications) that can be reasonably expected of the product by the buyer. When buying a rowboat, for example, you can expect it to be waterproof, but it would be unreasonable to demand that it be seaworthy during a raging storm.
With projects, however, it is not possible to be 100% certain at the start of the project as to what the exact end product will be. It is therefore difficult to formulate the exact specifications of the end project and to determine the ultimate quality. If the specifications of the end product are drawn up in detail, errors or ambiguities could arise, resulting in an end product that is not in accordance with these specifications and therefore of insufficient quality. Interim quality checks are therefore necessary when carrying out a project. It is usually the buyer or sponsor who determines whether some-thing is of sufficient quality. Quality costs money and high quality costs considerable money. In other words, you get what you pay for.
With many technical projects (building a ship, for example), the quality control criteria are likely to be readily available. A product can be assessed by measuring how much it deviates from the *specifications* laid down. If the   **Specifications**
margins that have been laid down – which could even be measured in tenths of millimetres – have not been exceeded, the product is of a sufficient quality.
In cases that are not as clear cut, the requirements should be formulated in such a way that the result is *measurable*. If a project has 'speeding up   **Measurable**

invoicing' as its goal, this is not measurable. "90% of the invoices should be sent within 2 days of shipping the goods" is, however. Also see section 1.12 on the SMART principles. The quality of all kinds of intermediate products is also measurable, whether it be the propeller of a ship or the completeness of the blueprint for the invoicing procedures mentioned in the last sentence.

Providing information and filing of documents (I)

Those working on the project should be kept well informed. Changes to the product specifications or major decisions relating to continuation of the project should be made known to those involved as soon as possible. If this is not done, the project workers may do unnecessary work based on superseded information. Parties such as the sponsor should also be kept informed.

Files   All documents written or collected during the project should be filed together. The files should be well ordered and accessible for all partici-pants, i.e. all relevant information should always be easily available.

Project archive   The *project archive* contains two types of documents:
- Documents with content-related information (working drawings, designs, products specifications, etc)
- Documents for managing the project to ensure efficiency and accounta-bility (agendas, minutes, schedules and the project plan).

Monitoring the project's objectives (O)

Things change all the time. If a sponsor wishes to make changes to the original objectives of the project, it is important that the project manager deals with this appropriately. A rigid project manager who discourages the **Changes**   sponsor from making *changes* to the project result might find that the end result is not optimal. On the other hand, if there are too many adjustments to the project this could unsettle things and impose a burden on the project members. This could have the effect of making the project unnecessarily long. If a project manager agrees to make a change to the project at the request of the sponsor, it must be realized that this could affect the deadlines. If these are not met and the sponsor forgets the request, this could cause problems. The wise project manager makes the – in terms of time as well as money – of any additions to the project clear to the sponsor in writing. The sponsor can then decide – as is his duty – whether the effect on costs and schedules warrants the proposed project changes. What frequently happens is that as soon as the consequences of a suggested alteration to the plans are made clear, it turns out not to be so desirable after all.

Change request   With large projects, an official *change request* must be submitted to the project manager before any changes to the project can be made. In addition to the desired changes, this request also contains reasoning, consequen-ces, costs and priority indication. The project manager then consults with the sponsor on the request and factors the consequences into the sche-dule and costs.

Threats to the project (O)

Getting off to a good start is no guarantee that the project will achieve its objectives. There are dangers at every turn, and it is up to the project manager to detect the signs. Some of the dangers are listed below:

- Initial enthusiasm among the team members, but waning as the project progresses. The project manager could try to remedy this by organizing communal activities that are not directly related to the job and that lift team morale.
- Unclear division of tasks within the team.
- Too much concern among the team members about what they themselves are getting out of the project.
- Differences of opinion and personal animosities making collaboration within the team difficult.
- The project's objectives remaining too vague or the specifications changing too often.
- The project manager tolerating too many adjustments.
- The decision process being too time consuming or not clear enough.
- Department managers even trying to undermine the project in order to get their staff back.
- Diminishing attention to the project being paid by the board of directors.

3.11 Why projects fail

To answer the question of why projects fail, we first have to decide when a project can be deemed successful.
A successful project is a project that:
- Has achieved its objectives (has delivered the project result) and is of the desired quality
- Is concluded in time
- Has not cost more than was agreed on

Projects frequently take longer to complete and cost more than originally planned. The project's objectives are also frequently only partly achieved. Some reasons for project failure have already been mentioned (in the previous section). Some others are given below (adapted from Blom & Storm 1993, Goldratt 1999 and Tumuscheit 1998).

Poor planning
If a project manager forgets to include a number of activities or materials, the project will turn out to be more expensive than planned. Before a wall can be built, the foundations need to be poured. Lack of experience in the building field might perhaps cause this to be overlooked. Delays can have a negative effect on the overall planning: if a big crane has not been hired well in advance and is therefore not available when it is needed, the rest of the building process may be delayed by it.
As Murphy's Law puts it: "If anything can go wrong, it will!" A variant does the rounds in the world of projects: "Murphy is alive and well – and working on your project!"
Planning is sometimes regarded as unnecessary. A relevant adage in this regard is "If you fail to plan, you are planning to fail". And while on the subject: "There are no good project managers – only lucky ones. The more you plan the luckier you get". If your plans are running behind schedule and you would like to speed thing up: "The bearing of a child takes nine months, no matter how many women are assigned to the project".

Too optimistic planning
Plans have a tendency to be too optimistic. The project manager needs to keep an eye on the project member who says, "I'll take care of that! Won't take me more than half a day!" The sponsor is frequently a professional optimist too: "Surely that can easily be done in two months!" One important cause of delays is very often the sponsor himself. He is responsible for making the decisions and a major cause of delay to projects is slowness in the decision-making process.

Failure to track progress
A good detailed schedule is often drawn up at the start of a project. As the project progresses, activities are carried out, but changes are often made to the initial schedule. Progress and changes need to be integrated into the schedule in order to keep it up to date. In many projects, the original schedule is either neglected or not updated enough.

Starting an activity too late
There is usually a certain amount of slack built into the schedules. Allowance is made in them for minor delays. If a project is started late, this slack is used up before the start and delays will be likely. This is sometimes referred to as the *"student effect"*, because students often ask for an extension of two weeks if they have to hand in an assignment in a week's time, but they often do not start on the assignment until the two weeks have expired.

Student effect

Project members are not competent enough
The project manager (or sponsor) is inexperienced and has inadequate leadership skills. The wrong decisions are made or decisions are made too late or even not at all. Being the content expert, the project manager becomes too concerned with the details and content of the project and too little with managing the project. Much is demanded of project managers (see section 2.5). However, while they are often chosen because they are experts in their field, an excellent technician is unlikely to be the person most capable of managing the project.
The project manager is likely to need project workers from within the organization. Department managers tend not to lend out those staff members most suitable for the project to work on the project because they are also the people that are the most useful within their own department and they want to keep them there.

The project is being sabotaged
If some people within an organization are disadvantaged by the project (or think they are) they may even try to sabotage the project out of self-interest. If new computer software is to be introduced in a department, the department manager might try to frustrate the project for fear of losing some of his staff.

Project members have too much on their plates
Project members who are not working on the project full-time – probably the majority – have to constantly switch from one task to another. If somebody needs three days to perform a task but he has to do many other things in between those three days can easily become three weeks. If there are only three days scheduled, then the project manager has a problem on his hands.

Project workers aiming at too much perfection

Computer programmers and technicians do work that is quite creative. They have a tendency to refine every detail of their work, since in a sense it is their own creation. There are always improvements that can be made to a computer program; technical solutions to a problem can be made just a little bit more elegant. This can sometimes be a cause of delay. Students tend to spend an exorbitant amount of time embellishing their thesis.

Stakeholders are insufficiently involved

To ensure the success of a project, it is important that all those involved in the project – the stakeholders – are (literally) involved in all activities. Projects often result in changes and, although most people are willing to make changes, they are not willing to be changed. If not enough time is invested in fostering trust, communication is poor or wrong expectations are built up on the part of the various stakeholders, the project will probably fail.

Little delays all add up

If minor project details are constantly subjected to delays and little extras have to be paid for, the result may very well be that the project as a whole will suffer major delays and will cost far more than originally planned.

Late delivery of purchased materials

A project's dependence on the delivery of materials by outside suppliers can be a source of delay. It is important to select suppliers not only on the basis of prices, but also on their ability to deliver the goods on time. The extra costs involved in a project being delayed may far outweigh the costs involved in selecting a somewhat more expensive but reliable supplier.

No provision for rectifying mistakes

Mistakes made during the course of a project have to be rectified. Rectification could turn out to be very costly. If the foundations of a house prove not to be solid enough, part of the house might have to be torn down. When making a budget and a project plan, provision should be made for rectification of mistakes.

Ignoring preliminary and finishing off activities

Work on a project never consists 100% of the activity itself; there are always preliminary activities involved. Before a wall is built, the bricks have to be carted to the actual site of the wall. After the wall has been erected all the rubble and rubbish has to be carted off. If the preliminary and finishing up activities are not included in the schedules, the project will take longer than expected.

Calamities

Unforeseen calamities (disasters) can cause the project to fail. If, for example, the walls of a house under construction blow down during a storm or a freak wind blows the roof off, the project will be delayed as a result of this calamity.

Unclear objectives

The ultimate goals of a project should be clear to all involved in it. All too often this is not the case. The sponsor sometimes does not know exactly

what he wants or is not able to explain it adequately to the project manager. Naturally the project's objectives must be in keeping with the objectives
of the organization as a whole.

Changes of definition

Changing the project's objectives – either wholly or in part – during the
execution of the project is termed a change of definition. A building
contractor asked to add an extra room during the actual building of the
house is unlikely to agree to the request there and then. He will only agree
if the budget and the schedules are adjusted accordingly. The house will
become more expensive and will be finished later than originally planned.
This is a frequent situation in the building trade.
In projects whose objective it is to alter organizations (via staff reorganiza-
tions, the introduction of computer systems, improved logistics and so on),
it is common for the terms to be changed without any alteration to the
budget or the time involved. This often causes projects to become more
imperceptibly expensive and delayed.
In software development projects, the sponsor will often suddenly come to
the conclusion that the program has to work in a different way than agreed
on. While it is easy to have a mental picture of a house that is going to be
built, it is much more difficult to picture how a computer program will work.
Consequently, such projects are prone to changes to their plans. A good
project manager has the sponsor and others submit a written *change
request* about the consequences in terms of time and money of the desired
alterations to the plans.

**Change
request**

The changing world

If the duration of a project is extremely long, the world may have changed
quite a bit before the project is completed. This may mean that the
project's objectives have to be adjusted. It is consequently advisable to
divide large or lengthy projects into phases. The plans can then be adjusted
at the conclusion of each phase. The changes that inevitably take place
during the course of time also mean that short-term projects are usually
preferred, as long-term projects run too much risk.
During the 1960s, many companies invested large sums of money in
immensely complex computer programs aimed at completely computerizing
the company. These projects sometimes lasted more than five years.
Developments in the outside world often meant that the program was
useless by the time it was finally installed. Nowadays, it is customary to
require that computer projects completed within one year.

Interest costs

Projects often involve massive investments. The necessary finances usually
have to be borrowed or made available through the organization's own
resources. This entails a loss of interest and, in large projects, the loss can
amount to such a high sum that if there is a delay the profitability of the
project will be severely affected. The building of the tunnel under the
English Channel involved enormous sums of money. Because the project
was late in finishing the interest that had to be paid increased considerably. Extra money had to be borrowed to meet the interest costs, which in
turn meant that the financial benefits of the project started to come in
much later than planned.

3.12   Project risks

A number of factors were mentioned in the last section that can cause a project to fail. These issues pose a risk for the success of the project. Every project entails risks. This section maps out the most important risks in a structured manner by means of a *risk analysis* and provides possible solutions.

Risk analysis

Risk

What is a risk exactly? A risk is the possibility of suffering harm or loss due to an undesirable event. A risk is based on the likelihood of the event occurring and the consequences of that event.

$$\text{Size of risk} = \text{Likelihood of occurrence} \times \text{Consequence for project}$$

The *likelihood* lies between 0 and 1, with 1 being the absolutely certainty that the event will occur and 0 being absolute certainty that the event will not occur. Instead of 0 and 1, the likelihood can also be shown in terms of a percentage: 0% and 100%. The *consequence* (impact or effect) for the project is the maximum harm that would occur if the risk becomes a fact. A high likelihood percentage does not necessarily represent a major risk. After all, if the likelihood of an event is reasonably high, but the negative consequence very minor, the risk is probably not very great. If the conse-quence is significant – such as the burning down of a company building – a minor likelihood can still lead to a risk that prompts the organization to take out insurance against this risk.

Likelihood

Consequence

A risk-conscious project manager carries out a risk analysis of his project before getting started.

Project risks

Section 3.10 lists a number of possible risks. Below, important project risks are broken down into various focal areas (according to Heerkens 2002):

- **Size of project** (scope): the project assignment is unclear, the desired project result is unclear, the sponsor keeps coming up with new roles, the project assignment changes during the project, the amount of work is difficult to estimate.
- **Project planning**: the turnaround time is underestimated, setbacks are not taken into account, the final date is postponed or unrealistic, the decision-making process is too long.
- **Market** (for commercial projects): unrealistic user or sponsor expecta-tions, market changes in the interim, prices or selling quantities change.
- **Materials**: poor availability, unreliable materials and suppliers, poor quality, high prices.
- **Facilities and tools**: poor availability, unreliable, incompatible with other tools, too few or unsuitable, not available in the right place.
- **People** (project members, personnel, interpersonal): project members change, unclear hourly rates, limited availability of project members, misplaced priorities, project members that 'flee' from the project, job openings, illness, family problems, conflicting interests, ethical ques-tions, poor performance, conflict, poor motivation and attitude, insuffi-ciently competent project members, incompetent sponsor.

- **Organization**: unclear division of roles and responsibilities, poor relationship between different stakeholders, insufficient coordination, political games, poor communication, conflict of interest between line management and project management.
- **External influences**: poor weather, natural disaster, (new) government regulations, health risk or regulations, patents, cultural differences, political instability, economic malaise, poor image, lawsuits.

Risk analysis

Carrying out a risk analysis makes the risks more visible and easier to discuss. This analysis is an excellent tool for looking ahead. It is carried out as follows:

1 Take stock of risks

Try to obtain an accurate and comprehensive picture of the project risks that threaten your project. You can do this through, for example, brainstorming. You can also inquire into the causes and what kinds of actions have already been taken to avoid these risks.

2 Analyze the risks

After taking stock of the risks, you need to analyze them. The various methods that can be used are not discussed here in any detail. The following is the global process for every project risk identified:

- Examine the causes of the possible risk. If the risk is a simple one, you can do this 'by feel'. A "herringbone diagram" can be used for more complicated risks. This analysis method is not covered here, but can easily be found online.
- Estimate the likelihood of the risky event occurring.
- Estimate the maximum harm (consequence) of the event if it occurs.

Next, draw up a list of the most important risks in order of priority. When determining measures to be taken, you will have to give precedence to those risks with the highest priority. The relevant risks, likelihood of them occurring, maximum scope of the damage and priority are all included on the risk list. Now that you have an idea of the greatest risks relevant to your project, you can determine the necessary measures in response.

3 Formulate measures

Using the above list, determine together with the sponsor which measures are possible and what they will cost. Next, make a list of priorities. There are several approaches to dealing with risks:

- **Preventative**. You take measures to avoid the risk: you eliminate the risk by omitting certain activities or choosing a different solution.
- **Repressive**. You take measures to reduce the risk: you limit the possibility of damage or the extent of the damage.
- **Transference**. You take measures to transfer the risk: you have someone else assume the risk, such as a supplier or insurance company. This usually involves a cost. If you have part or all of the project carried out by a supplier in a structural manner, this is called **contracting out** or **outsourcing**. The supplier essentially runs the risks for the activities that have been outsourced. Keep in mind that, should something go wrong at your supplier's, you may still be affected by it.
- **Acceptance**. You accept the risk and do not take any measures.

Your project plan should contain a separate chapter devoted to the risk analysis (see Chapter 5). To carry out a more detailed risk analysis for a company or project, the book *Zo doe je een risicoanalyse* (Gerritsma/Grit, 2009) can be of help.

3.13 Terminating a project prematurely

If a project is in danger of failing, the following argument is often given: "We can't stop the project because 100,000 dollars has already been invested in it". This is a non-argument. If a project must ultimately result in a profit or *savings* (asset), it is essential to know the cost of the project at a particular point in time and how much the ultimate expected profit will be.

Savings

By way of example, Table 3.1 makes a comparison of three commercial projects for which $100,000 is invested at a particular point in time (T). The profit at the end of each of the projects is $250,000. For projects 1, 2 and 3, another $100,000, $200,000 and $300,000, respectively, must be invested at a particular point in time in order to achieve this profit. Project 1 is ultimately successful, whereas projects 2 and 3 are not. But, as you can see, project 3 must be terminated at a particular point in time, but not project 2. After all, another $200,000 must be invested in project 2 in order to make a profit of $250,000. These are the positive results at that particular point in time. However, project 2 is not a success in its entirety due to the loss of $50,000 during the total project period.

TABLE 3.1 Stop or don't stop?

	Project 1	Project 2	Project 3
Already invested by deadline (T)	$100,000	$100,000	$100,000
Still to be invested by deadline (T)	$100,000	$200,000	$300,000
Profit at end of project	$250,000	$250,000	$250,000
Continue/stop at deadline (T)?	Yes	Yes	No
Total project results at end of project	+$50,000	–$50,000	–$50,000
Successful project?	Yes	No	No

To put it simply, the project should have more profit than loss at every point in time. Unfortunately, the reality is a lot more complex since the termination of a project can itself have a cost. If, for example, a construction project is terminated prematurely, the structures already built will have to be torn down, which can be quite costly. And, since the termination of a project is also often considered a loss of face for the sponsor or project manager, most projects are simply continued regardless.

Assignments

3.1 What are three types of company that frequently work on projects?

3.2 What is a pilot project? Give two reasons why an organization would run a pilot project.

3.3
  a What is a kick-off meeting?
  b What is another name for a kick-off meeting?
  c What are three objectives of a kick-off meeting?

3.4 Why write a project proposal? During which phase of the project should this be done?

3.5 Write a project proposal for the following situations:
  a You want to organize a graduation party for your department and you need management cooperation and funding.
  b You want to organize a three-day outing in your area of expertise for your department or company and you need management cooperation and funding.

3.6 What is the difference between a project proposal and a project plan?

3.7 In your own words, describe the significance of each of the five monitoring aspects of a project.

3.8 Which of the five monitoring aspects should the project manager of a manned space flight pay the most attention to? Explain your answer.

3.9 A project requires a budget.
  a What is understood by the term "budget"?
  b Who makes the budget available?
  c What does he get in return?
  d How is the project budget spent??
  e How can the budget be monitored during the execution of the project?

3.10 Quality is one of the five aspects of a project.
  a In your own words, explain what is understood by the "quality of a project".
  b Who determines whether the product is of sufficient quality?
  c "The quality must be as high as possible!" How would you respond to this statement?

3.11 A sponsor wants to have a project carried out. What is the difference for the sponsor between buying a company car and "buying" a project outcome?

3.12   Which two kinds of documents are found in a project archive? Give two examples of each.

3.13   **a** What is likely to happen if the project workers receive insufficient information from the project manager?
b Quality control is easier in technical projects than in reorganization projects. Explain why this is the case.

3.14   **a** What is the danger of a project manager going along with too many of the sponsor's requests to alter the project?
b What is the danger of the project manager not allowing any changes at all?
c Why should a project manager demand that the sponsor put down any alterations to the project's objective in writing?

3.15   Quality should be measurable. Suggest a number of criteria that can be used to measure the quality of the following projects (i.e. when they can be regarded as successful).
a A project for collecting money for third-world countries
b An ideal home fair
c A thesis project
d An conference on the environment
e An excursion
f A computerization project for the introduction of new software
g Building a bridge

3.16   What is the risk if the stakeholders are not sufficiently involved in the execution of a project?

3.17   Respond to the following statement: "We can't terminate this project because $50,000 has already been invested in it."

3.18   At the conclusion of a project, its success can be determined by testing the quality of the end product (the project results). While the duration of a project could be up to a year, to avoid the risk of receiving an unsatisfactory end product, the sponsor is unlikely to leave the assessment until then. He will want to assess the intermediate products.
a For each of the projects mentioned in assignment **3.15**, list a number of intermediate products.
b For each of these intermediate products, show how their quality could be assessed.

3.19   Discuss the following statements in groups:
a It is best to postpone major items of expenditure until as late in the project as possible.
b The quality of both an intermediate and end product of a project should be as high as possible.
c Making a project plan improves the chances of creating a high-quality product.
d Not only is planning of the manpower involved in a project necessary, but also planning of the financial costs.

3.20   The following example (based on Tumuscheit, 1998) demonstrates how
things can go very wrong in the early stages of a project.
A top manager in your company has a problem and he asks you to be his
project manager. In your enthusiasm and because you feel flattered to have
been asked, you agree to take on the task. When you get back home you
realize that you have a number of problems on your hands.
- It is not quite clear exactly what the manager wants you to do. It turns
  out later on that the manager himself does not know exactly either.
  Worse is to come: as the project proceeds, it becomes clear that the
  manager wants you to resolve a problem that is not the real problem at
  all. The project's objectives are unclear and you do not know what the
  outcomes of the project are supposed to be.
- As well as this, your manager's budget has almost run out and consequently the project has to cost as little as possible. Moreover, you are
  unclear about what has to be done and the deadline is impossibly short.
- Getting the others to collaborate properly is proving virtually impossible.
  Everybody within the company is extremely busy, and the department
  managers need all the personnel they have and are not prepared to let
  you have their staff members – and certainly not their best ones!
- The next problem relates to your own lack of experience. How should you
  approach the project? What is your first step? What happens then, and
  how are you going to get others to collaborate with you?

Discuss in groups how this situation could best be dealt with.

project

4
Planning and scheduling

Planning of activities is essential to efficient work. Whatever the project, it must be well planned, and these plans must be properly scheduled. Inadequate planning of large building projects could even cause the project to run at a loss.

This chapter describes techniques for planning and scheduling.

4.1 Why plan?

Planning is done for the following reasons:
- To determine the **duration** (total turnaround time) of a project. The project activities are either planned in reverse order with the finishing date of a project as the basis, or done on the basis of the project's starting date, with the duration of a project worked out from there.
- To determine what the **consequences of delay** are likely to be on the duration of the project as a whole. While delay in some activities will have no bearing on the duration, delay in other activities will cause the entire project to be delayed.
- To **determine the costs** of a project. The deployment of manpower and resources can be expressed as a cost factor via hourly rates and cost price.

Organize
activities
- To *organize* the *activities* of the project workers. This is one way of determining what has to be done and the amount of time available to do so.

Monitor
progress
- To *monitor* the *progress* of a project. What has been achieved so far and how much of the budget has been used up?

4.2 Concepts and terms

The following are common planning concepts:
- An **activity** or **task** is the amount of work that needs to be done during the course of a project. In this book, the terms "task" and "activity" or "project activity" refer to the same thing.
- The **duration** of an activity is the time that elapses between the commencement and completion of the project. The terms should not be confused with time spent on the activity: an activity that starts on the Wednesday of one week and finishes on the following Tuesday has a duration of 7 days (if your working time is 7 days a week).
- The **required working hours** are all the working hours necessary to complete the job. If four people each work eight hours on an activity on a given day, then the required working hours are $4 \times 8 = 32$ hours. The required working hours are multiplied by the hourly rates to ascertain the costs of a project.
- If an activity is not finished on schedule, this is called a **delay**. An activity has a one-day delay if, according to the schedule, it should have been done yesterday, but was not finished until today.
- A **milestone** is an intermediate product that is produced during the duration of a project. The end of an activity or a group of activities can be a milestone. It is important to have sufficient milestones because they can serve as measuring points to monitor progress. If a milestone is not reached on the planned date there will be a delay.
- A **dependent activity** can only be carried out after completion of another activity. A dependent task is said to be linked to its predecessor. Filling a pool with water has to be preceded by making the pool waterproof. Some activities must be carried out at a set time.
- A **critical activity** is an activity whose duration will affect the duration of the project as a whole.
- A **critical path** is a chain of critical activities. Those activities not on the critical path have some **slack** to them. Activities on the critical path have

no slack and any delay will delay the whole project. Generally speaking, there is one critical path in a schedule at one particular point in time. In unusual cases, there might be two or more critical paths, but all of them are equal in length. If activities that are not on the critical path are delayed, the critical path might change.
- A non-critical activity is an activity with a certain amount of slack. This slack can be used in several ways: the activity could be carried out as soon as possible (**ASAP**) or as late as possible (**ALAP**). Spending large sums of money during a project will usually be postponed to the last moment. It is also possible to spread an activity that has some slack over the entire time span available. Note: An activity that is carried out As Late As Possible loses its slack and becomes a critical activity.
- The **resources** of a project are:
  1 The people who carry out the work
  2 The materials used during the activity and the tools necessary to carry out the activity.
- Scheduling can be quite tricky. A number of **scheduling techniques** have been developed during the course of time. The two most important ones are dealt with in the next two sections:
  1 Gantt charts
  2 Network diagrams

A few other common scheduling terms can be found in Section 4.9, which deals with the use of planning software.

4.3 Gantt charts

Scheduling can be a complicated and time-consuming business and this no doubt explains why people have devised ways and means to simplify the task. In this section, Gantt charts, also known as *bar charts* or time flow charts, are described.

Bar charts

On a Gantt chart, activities are indicated by strips or bars. One can see at a glance in what order activities have to take place and the duration of each activity. A Gantt chart can be drawn by hand.
It is also possible to use a *planning board* and strips of paper to make a Gantt chart. They can also be made by using a computer program. Figure 4.1 shows an example of a Gantt chart.

Planning board

FIGURE 4.1 Building information system Gantt Chart

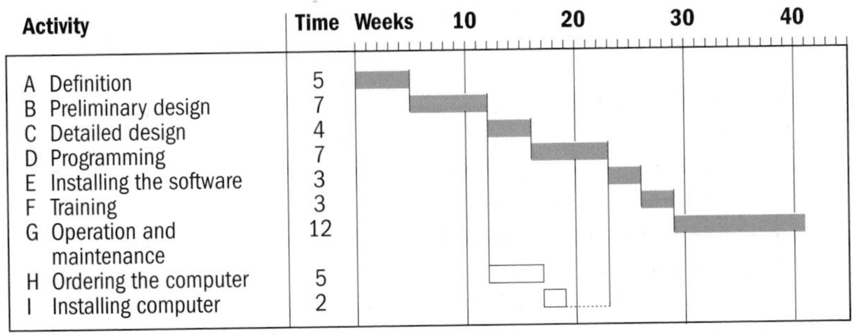

Activity	Time Weeks
A Definition	5
B Preliminary design	7
C Detailed design	4
D Programming	7
E Installing the software	3
F Training	3
G Operation and maintenance	12
H Ordering the computer	5
I Installing computer	2

Details of a Gantt chart

A simple Gantt chart contains the following parts:

- The **activity** is indicated by a strip or a bar. The length of the strip indicates the duration of the activity. If an activity is on the critical path it is highlighted in some way (by making it darker, for example).
- Any **slack** can be indicated by dotted lines.
- If desired, mutual **dependencies** can be linked by vertical lines in the chart. These activities can only be done after other activities have finished.

Features of a Gantt chart

A Gantt chart has the following features:

- The length of the strip provides an indication of the duration. It makes a Gantt chart orderly and easy to understand.
- A Gantt chart shows when an activity should start and when it should finish.
- Once it is made, a Gantt chart is awkward to change manually. If an activity takes longer than planned, all the subsequent strips on the planning board will have to be moved. A hand-drawn Gantt chart will most likely have to be drawn all over again.
- A *Gantt chart* could give the impression that certain activities have to be carried out in succession. This may not be the case. Apparently dependent activities may well be independent of each other.

An example of a Gantt chart

The owner of a sandwich bar wants to modernize his shop. He wants to alter his "business formula", and this involves structural alterations to the shop. The activities that have to be carried out are listed in Table 4.1.

TABLE 4.1 Table of activities involved in changing the business formula

Code	Description	Weeks	Can only take place after:
A	Conceptualize the formula	5	–
B	Look for architect	3	A
C	Look for building contractor	1	A
D	Create design	5	B
E	Rebuild	15	C, D
F	Redecorate	2	E
G	Do the finishing touches	1	F
H	Organize advertising	4	D
I	Reopen shop	1	G, H

Table of activities

Every activity in the *table of activities* is given a code and a description. The duration of each activity is stipulated. The dependencies are noted in the last column. Here, it is obvious that activity B can only be done after activity A is finished. Likewise, activity E can only be started after completion of both C and D.

Figure 4.2 shows the Gantt chart belonging to Table 4.1.

FIGURE 4.2 Changing a business formula Gantt chart

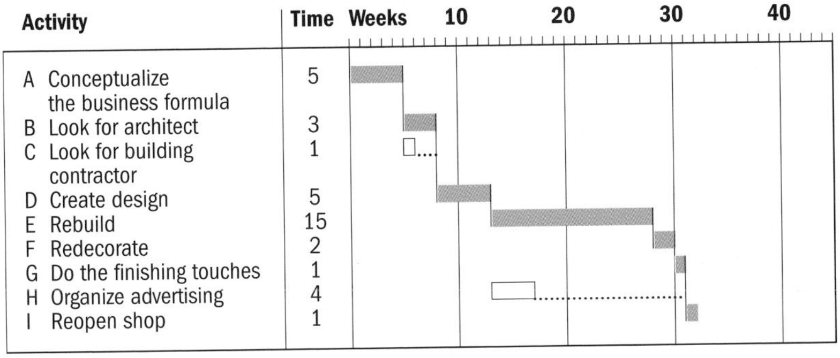

Activity	Time Weeks	10	20	30	40
A Conceptualize the business formula	5				
B Look for architect	3				
C Look for building contractor	1				
D Create design	5				
E Rebuild	15				
F Redecorate	2				
G Do the finishing touches	1				
H Organize advertising	4				
I Reopen shop	1				

You do not have to put the activities in the same order as in Fig. 4.2, but it provides a good overview. The critical path is the longest possible path and runs via the critical activities A-B-D-E-F-G-I. The reader is advised to take a close look at this.

When drawing up a table of activities, only the immediately preceding activities (predecessor) need be mentioned. If, as in Table 4.1, activity F follows D and D follows B then obviously B also precedes F. This dependency is not expressly shown in the table because it is already implied in the sequence F after D and D after B. Activities are sometimes represented as being dependent when this is not, in fact, the case. If they are defined as being dependent, the critical path will become longer than is necessary. Incidentally, there is slack after activities C and H in Figure 4.2.

4.4 Network diagrams

A network diagram is a tool for scheduling complicated projects involving multiple activities. The project does need to have a clear starting point and a clear finishing point. This section discusses the technique behind the network diagram and how to make one. Unless you are using a computer program, it times a lot of time to make an extensive network diagram. It does, however, give a good insight into the planning process. Planning programs on the computer have evolved from network diagrams. A network diagram (an example of which is shown in Fig. 4.3) can be used to draw up a Gantt chart.

Details of a network diagram
A network diagram consists of the following:
- A circle as starting point and as finishing point.
- Rectangles (or circles) used to indicate finished activities. These are the milestones.
- Arrows indicate the dependencies and also denote the activities. The duration is indicated above the arrow.

FIGURE 4.3 Network diagram

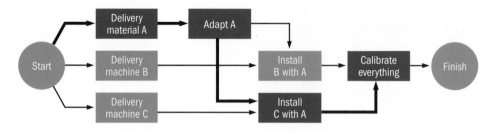

If an arrow is on the critical path it is drawn in bold. A milestone that lies on the critical path is also drawn as a bold rectangle. This book uses a variation on the *activity on arrow* method instead of the activity on node method. The arrow also represents the activity; the rectangle or circle (node) is a milestone.

Activity on arrow

Properties of a network diagram
Some properties of a network diagram are as follows:
- Dependencies between activities can be seen at a glance. These are indicated by arrows and there is one arrow per dependency.
- The length of the arrow has no bearing on the duration. You consequently cannot see at a glance how much time is involved.
- Having to change things by hand in a complicated network diagram is very time-consuming.

Instructions for drawing up a network diagram
- Start from the table of activities. Draw a circle to indicate the starting activity and label it "Start".
- Draw a rectangle for every activity that does not follow on from another activity. In the last column of the table of activities these are indicated by a dash.
- Starting from the circle, draw an arrow to each of these activities.
- Draw rectangles for all the other milestones and connect them to the preceding activity with an arrow. If there is more than one preceding activity, use arrows to connect each one.
- In the rectangles or circles indicate the activity's code.
- Above the arrows leading to an activity indicate the duration of this activity
- To determine the critical path, check the lengths of the various paths and their duration. The longest path will be the critical path.

Several methods can be used to determine the critical path of complicated network diagrams. These will not, however, be dealt with in this book. Those who have to make a large and complicated network diagram should use a computer program for that purpose (see section 4.8).

An example of a network diagram
A student has to submit a thesis as part of his final examination. The thesis must look professional and so it is essential that it be done on the computer. He does not have one, however, so he sets out to persuade his parents to let him buy one. He draws up a table of activities (see Table 4.2).

TABLE 4.2 Writing thesis: table of activities

Code	Activities	Days	Only possible after
A	Prepare thesis	12	–
B	Write draft version of thesis	21	A
C	Select and buy a PC	10	A
D	Install PC and learn to use it	13	C
E	Select word processor	4	A
F	Buy word processor	5	E
G	Install word processor on PC	1	D, F
H	Write thesis on PC	7	B, G

If the recommended procedure for making a network diagram is applied to this, it will look like Fig. 4.4.

FIGURE 4.4 Writing thesis network diagram

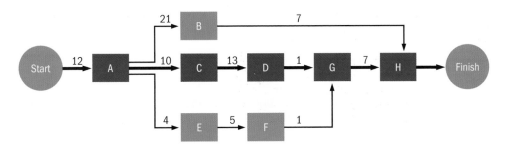

In order to determine the critical path, the lengths of all possible paths have to be calculated. This simple example has three paths from start to finish:
1 Path A-E-F-G-H takes 12 + 4 + 5 + 1 + 7 = 29 days
2 Path A-C-D-G-H takes 12 + 10 + 13 + 1 + 7 = 43 days
3 Path A-B-H takes 12 + 21 + 7 = 40 days

To carry out all the activities requires at least 43 days are needed. Path A-C-D-G-H is the critical path and is indicated in bold. If any one of the activities A, C, D, G, or H takes longer than planned, the entire project will take longer (the reader should check this for him or herself).
The longest path is the duration of the project. Sometimes the shortest way through the chart is regarded as the duration. Since every activity has to be carried out, this is not correct!

4.5 Deriving a Gantt chart from a network diagram

Once a network diagram has been drawn up, a Gantt chart can be derived from it:
- Firstly, a time scale is drawn up along the x-axis. This should be slightly longer than the duration of the project (the critical path which has been determined on the basis of the network diagram).
- Subsequently, strips should be drawn for all the activities that are on the critical path. Each strip has a length that is proportional to its duration. Care should be taken to let each activity start at the right moment. For the purposes of clarity, each strip could show the activity's code. The strips on the critical path should be drawn bolder than the others. Arranging the activities along the critical path from top left to bottom right gives the best impression.
- After this, the other activities can be included. These are the activities that are not part of the critical path and therefore have some slack. Those activities that are dependent should be taken into account and care should be taken to have them start at the right moment.
- For activities that are not on the critical path, any slack there is can be indicated by using dotted lines.
- Activity dependencies may be indicated by vertical lines

Fig. 4.5 shows the network diagram of the figure transformed into a Gantt chart in section 4.4. Study it carefully.

FIGURE 4.5 Writing thesis Gantt Chart

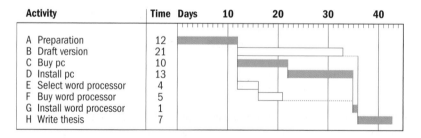

Activity	Time Days	10	20	30	40
A Preparation	12				
B Draft version	21				
C Buy pc	10				
D Install pc	13				
E Select word processor	4				
F Buy word processor	5				
G Install word processor	1				
H Write thesis	7				

4.6 Adjustments to schedules

After the schedules have been drawn up, they should be *monitored* during the course of the project to see whether the timing of the activities is proceeding according to schedule. To be able to do so, the project members need to report on their progress. They should hand in their time records to the project manager on a weekly basis. This is known as *progress reporting*. During the course of time some deviation from the original scheduling may become apparent. A schedule must therefore be adjustable. In the event of major alterations to the original schedules, they will have to be adjusted in consultation with the sponsor. Once a schedule

has been drawn up, it is not static (unchangeable), but dynamic (change-able).
The changes must be made known to all participants, and the project manager will need to report them to the sponsor. Lost time caused by small deviations from the schedules can sometimes be rectified by working overtime or bringing in additional manpower.
Some members of a project team will schedule very tightly to please the project manager and some very freely to create some free time for themsel-ves. Some will have no idea how long an activity will take. The project manager will therefore have to assess the schedules the project's partici-pants have drawn up on the basis of *how feasible they seem*: are they really achievable?

4.7 Which activities are required?

You have already determined the goal of your project and the end result. You also know how to draw up a schedule. Now you need to determine what *kinds of activities* and tasks should be carried out in order to achieve your end result. Since projects have a once-only objective by definition, there is a good chance that you have little to no experience in determining the exact activities needed for this particular project. So how can you figure out what needs to be done in order to carry out the project to completion? As you know, if you forget important tasks in the beginning, you will never be able to formulate a good schedule and will have little chance of getting the project finished in time.
To figure out what activities are needed, you can complete the following steps:

Kinds of activities

1 Come up with as many different activities as possible. Try to derive these from the end product.
2 Consult relevant literature or try to get hold of a schedule from a similar project.
3 Consult with your (future) project team mates.
4 Interview an experienced project manager.
5 Consult with the sponsor.
6 Create a Work Breakdown Structure.

A *Work Breakdown Structure* (abbreviated as WBS) contains a schematic overview of project activities. It is a tool that is used to organize not only project activities but also your thoughts and ideas. An example – albeit incomplete – is shown in Figure 4.6. The diagram is structured from high level to detail level, with the details at the bottom. You can try to place all activities in a single diagram or, if the structure is much larger, subdivide it. In the example given here, everything from the "market research" square can be placed in a separate WBS. The "market research" square is then placed in the first WBS as well as at the top of the second (subdivided) WBS.

Work Breakdown Structure

FIGURE 4.6 A Work Breakdown Structure

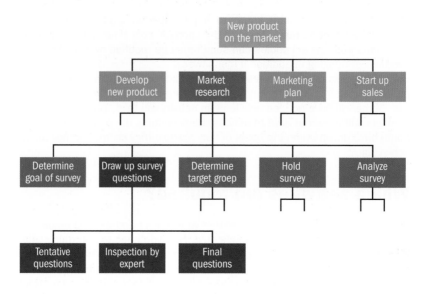

A completed WBS can be easily entered into a planning program on the computer.

4.8 Planning software

Spreadsheet
Planning
software

A computer can be used for the scheduling process. *Spreadsheet* programs may be used or a specially designed *planning software* for making Gantt charts. A spreadsheet program is not very suitable for large projects, and it will not be dealt with here.

There is a great deal of reasonably priced, user-friendly planning software for PCs on the market now.

Some of the possibilities opened up by planning software are as follows:
- It is possible to draw up a Gantt chart and a network diagram from the same planning data.
- Activities can be grouped into project phases.
- Activities and duration can be put into the program very easily.
- Dependencies between activities can easily be registered (simply by clicking the mouse).
- Manpower and resources can be assigned to activities. The required workload can be put into the program.
- The schedules can be calculated fully automatically.
- Resource rates can be entered, enabling automatic calculation of costs.
- The program can indicate where the problem areas are.
- The progress of the project can be monitored. When changes are made the schedules can easily be recalculated.
- Working times and resource availability can be included using the calendar function.

One disadvantage of the manual network and Gantt charts described in the previous sections is that they cannot take into account the availability of resources. Only the duration of a project can be planned with them. There is no way of telling whether at any given moment the required personnel and resources are available to carry out the activity. A delay of one day in one activity could, in practice, mean a total delay of three weeks if, for example, the activity was planned to be completed on the very last day before vacation. Planning software can take such things into account. Planning software incorporates a number of *calendar functions* that enable such calculations to be made:

Calendar functions

- A general calendar option for the whole of the company
- A calendar option for the project
- A separate calendar option for each participant and each resource

The days and hours that people and resources are available (the working times) can be noted using the calendar function. For example, public holidays, the weekends, vacations and other days off can be put into the program per company, project or staff member. An automatic planner takes account of all of these.

Monitoring the progress of the project is another possibility. If required, the program can produce a list of activities for every staff member. These can be handed out and can contain the activities that the staff member has to perform during the coming week. This can also serve as a means for the staff member to record his own progress on the task. He could hand this list in to his project manager once a week and the project manager could then feed the data into the computer. This way a new set of schedules can be produced each week. Planning software can be used for reviews of budget expenditure, progress and deployment of resources.

Progress project

For people who have to plan a lot, it is very worthwhile to acquire and learn to use a planning software package. To enable workers within the same organization to fit in with each others' schedules, the same planning software should be used by all concerned. If a company has not yet specified which type, it is best to confer with other planners within the organization to agree on the software to be used.

Standard

4.9 Using planning software

This section will deal with practical applications of planning software. It will describe how to use such software, explain some terms relating to planning programs and briefly describe how to draw up a planning chart. Since it takes time to learn how to use planning software, readers who do not intend to work with such software can skip this section.

Frequently used planning programs are Microsoft Project, CA-SuperProject, Time Line, Project Scheduler and TurboProject Professional.

Getting started with planning software

To learn how to plan your schedules with the help of planning software, follow the following instructions one by one:

- First, read through this section. The basic terminology is explained here.
- Follow the "Getting started" or "Quick preview" instructions of your software's "Help" section.
- Make a simple Gantt chart. Fig. 4.7 shows a screen print of such a chart. This one was made with MS Project.

- Examples of schedules are usually given in planning software. These should be studied carefully.
- Make ample use of the "Help" section of the software. Carefully read the text balloons that appear when you let your cursor rest on an item for a while.
- Double-clicking and using the right-hand mouse button often brings up useful functions and possibilities. Take time to explore the possibilities of the program. Look at the menu screens and try and master the program in this way.

FIGURE 4.7 Screen print of a Gantt Chart

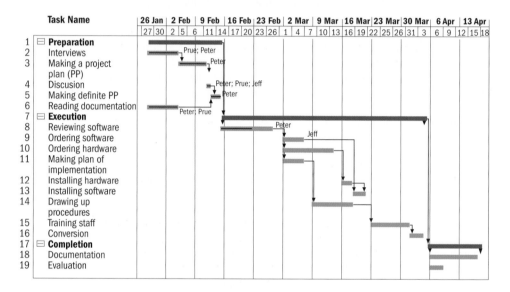

Buying a program handbook or doing a course to become more familiar with the planning software are other options. If you have to plan regularly, this is highly recommended.

 The "Mini course on MS Project" can be downloaded from the website accompanying this book. If you do not have MS Project, the "Planning" spreadsheet model can be downloaded for use in creating a simple Gantt chart.

Levels of planning programs

Planning software can be used to make a plan or a schedule on various levels:

- As a drawing kit for a network diagram (PERT chart) and attractive Gantt chart. The result is a graphic representation of the activities or tasks to be carried out and inter-dependencies of the tasks. The graphic representations can be used during consultations with the sponsor.
  A computer-drawn Gantt chart can be added to your project plan.
- For assigning or allocating activities to persons and resources. You can then use the program to show your staff when they will be called upon to do certain tasks.

- For recording the activities that have been completed. By introducing the finished and partly finished activities into the program you can monitor the progress of the project. Is everything still on track; how far are we behind? You could indicate in the planning software what percentage of each task has been completed.
- For comparing adapted schedules with an earlier or the original schedule. For this purpose, the so-called baselines of a certain moment in time should be saved. The present plan is then compared with that baseline. This procedure is called tracking.
- For financial analyses. How much money – what sort of budget – do I need for carrying out this project? How much has been spent already? Each resource can be linked to an hourly rate or a set rate, enabling a financial schedule to be made and monitored.

Under the heading "Working times" the availability of resources can be recorded using the calendar function. It is also possible to record the working times for the project as a whole using the project calendar function. When a plan is drawn up, these working times are then automatically taken into account.

Planning software allows presentation on screen of the same data organized in various ways, including as the following:

- Gantt chart   time flow chart
- PERT chart   network diagram
- Tracking   comparison of performance to earlier schedules (tracking)
- Resources   how they are deployed. You can easily see when resources are used in the Resource view, as well as how much time was spent and the cost
- Calendar   tasks and/or resources are recorded on a calendar. You can then see which activity has to be carried out on any given day and who has to do it.

Procedure for making a schedule

The following method may be used to make a schedule. Steps *a* to *e* can also be used when making a schedule manually.

a Decide on a starting date or a finishing date for your project (or both). It is sometimes possible to begin with a starting date and from that point determine the finishing date, but if the finishing date is fixed, the scheduling should be done in reverse.

b Make a list of the tasks that have to be carried out. The list should be as detailed as possible and the tasks organized in groups and phases.

c Estimate the duration of each task. It may be wise to consult the person performing the task or consult an expert.

d Assign the right resources to each task: workers with the right capacities or the required tools and materials. Keep the availability of the resources in mind.

e Determine the dependencies: what activities can only be performed if others have been completed? A task that has to be finished before another can be started is known as a *predecessor*. A task can have several predecessors. A task that is carried out after completion of another is called a *successor*.

The dependency between two tasks (A and B) can take various forms:
- Finish to start: task B can only be started after task A is finished
- Start to start: task B can only be started after task A has been started
- Finish to finish: task B cannot be finished before task A is finished
- Start to finish: task B cannot be finished before task A is started

The most common dependency is of the type *finish to start*.
- f   Insert your data into the computer program
- g   Print the required reviews. Modern planning software includes the option of exporting reports as Internet pages, making printing unnecessary: every participant in the project can see the project reports by using a browser program such as Internet Explorer or Netscape Navigator.

Automatic planning

Program planning can be done automatically. A task can be planned as early or as late as desired. It is also possible to put a constraint on a task. We therefore have the following options:
- As soon as possible: this is the standard option when scheduling from a starting date
- As late as possible: could be used when a project is planned in reverse from the finishing date
- Finish no earlier than: a task must not be completed before a set date
- Finish no later than: a task must be completed before a set date
- Must finish on: a task must be completed on an exact date
- Must start on: a task must be started on an exact date
- Start no earlier than: a task should not be started before a set date
- Start no later than: a task should not be started later than a set date

What if

Since the effect of any alteration in the plans can be calculated immediately, a "*what if*" calculation can be made: an alteration is made to the plan and the effect is calculated. An optimistic, a realistic or a pessimistic estimate of the duration of a task could be made. The planning software will tell you if something is technically not possible. If you assign so many tasks to a worker that he will have to work 36 hours a day, the program will point that out to you.

Other terms

The following terms are frequently used in planning software:

Lag time

Lag time. This is the necessary time interval between two dependent tasks. Between the dependent activities of building a brick wall and placing window frames there will be a lag time – in this case, the time it takes for mortar to dry thoroughly – of three days. See Figure 4.8.

Lead time

Lead time. If there is a partial overlap in time between two dependencies, lead time is planned in. The second activity may be started before the first activity is completely finished. Lag time is expressed in positive units (for example, +2 days); lead time is expressed in negative units. A lead time of −2 days indicates a two-day overlap.

In other words, a new task can be started before the previous task has been completed. For example, the task of "clearing the building site" can be started before the task of "building the house" is finished. See Figure 4.8. Lead time can also be translated as "overlap time". Since lead time is expressed in negative units, if two activities have a lead time of 2 days, you could call this a lag time of −2 days.

FIGURE 4.8 Lag time and lead time

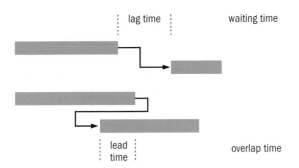

Priority. If there are not enough resources to carry out all tasks, your automatic planning will run into problems. A task priority rating (high, low) indicates which task should be scheduled first. — **Priority**

Effort driven. A task that is effort driven will take half the time if twice as many resources are deployed. — **Effort driven**

Fixed duration. Even if the resources are increased, a task that is scheduled to have a fixed duration will take just as long. If twice the number of human resources is deployed, each will only have to work on the task for 50% of the time. — **Fixed duration**

Milestone. A milestone is an important point in time: something reached on a set date. Milestones are included for the purposes of measuring the progress of a project. A milestone has a time duration of zero. — **Milestone**

Recurring task. This is a task that is repeated during the duration of a project: for example, every Monday for the next ten weeks a two-hour meeting starting at 10 a.m. for all team members. These tasks can be automatically recorded in the schedules by using the recurring task option. — **Recurring task**

4.10 Planning a large project in phases

There are a number of steps to planning a big project. These steps are outlined in Fig. 4.9 and described in detail in points 1 to 7 below.

FIGURE 4.9 Planning a large project

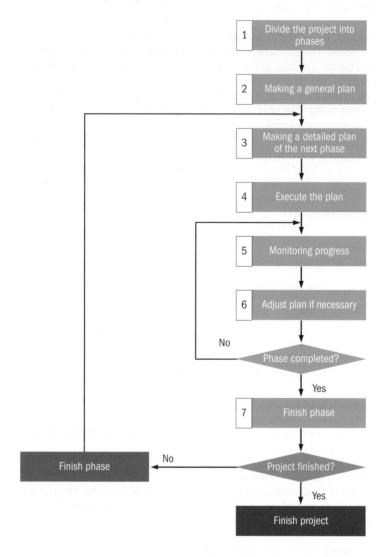

This is explained in more detail under points 1 through 7 below.

1 Divide the project into a number of phases
Dividing the project up into logical phases helps to keep the project clear and manageable. It is essential in big projects and advisable in smaller projects. At the end of each phase, the management team decides how to proceed further.
A useful way of dividing up a big project is according to the following phases:
• Concept: the idea that sparks it off
• Definition: defining what needs to be done
• Preliminary design: deciding how to go about it
• Detailed design: detailing how to do it

- Production: doing it
- Aftercare: making it operational and providing aftercare.

These phases have been described in detail in Chapter 1. In a small project, you can usually make do with the phases *detailed design*, *production* and *aftercare*.

2   Make a general plan for the whole of the project
It is not realistic for the sponsor to demand a detailed plan for the whole of the project at its commencement. A general plan ought to be sufficient at this stage.

3   Make a detailed plan for the following phase
A detailed plan for the next phase can be made. Since this phase is to be executed shortly, an overview should be possible.

Collect all the *data* needed to plan the next phase.   **Data**
- List as many of the tasks that have to be done as possible
- Arrange the tasks in logical groups
- Determine the dependencies between the groups and tasks: what tasks can only be done after other tasks are finished?
- Determine the duration of each task.

Make time and *activity schedules*. These should be thoroughly discussed   **Activity**
with the project workers. They themselves will usually know best what   **schedules**
activities have to be carried out and what time and resources are required.
The overall scheduling should, of course, also be discussed with the
sponsor.

4   Put the plans into action
The tasks are carried out by the project workers. It is the project manager's job to coordinate the tasks.

5   Collect data relating to progress
Time registration is an essential part of the progress report. The project   **Time**
workers should render an account of the time spent on the various tasks.   **registration**
They should also indicate any deviation from the original plans they expect
will be necessary. It is up to the project workers and the project manager to
ensure the quality of the expected results.

6   Adjust the schedules if necessary
If the progress data and the project workers indicate that there are likely to be major changes to the plans, the schedules will have to be adjusted. These adjustments should be discussed with the sponsor. Small deviations from the times schedules can be alleviated by such measures as working overtime. After the schedules have been altered, all of the project's members will need to receive a copy of the new plan. If there is a delay in completing this phase, go back to point 4.

7   Finish the phase
When a phase is completely finished it should be formally rounded off. A decision then needs to be made about whether to continue, and if so, how. For this purpose a management summary (see Chapter 11) could be made.

If necessary the general plan (point 2) can be adjusted. When there is more clarity about how to continue, a detailed plan can be made for the next phase (back to point 3).

4.11 Time management

It is strange fact, but while some people can get immense amounts of work done, others find it hard to make headway. Having said this, there is, however, never enough time, not only for project work. This section will give some suggestions for effective *time management*.

Time management

- Always start the day by making a list of tasks. It will take about ten minutes to do and might save you a lot of time. Buy a large diary and write the list in it. You can also write a list in your mobile phone.
- Jot down all the tasks and put a minus sign (–) in front of each point. When the task is completed, make the sign into a plus sign (+). Work on changing all the minuses into plusses. At the end of the day you will find it easy to see where your time went.
- Note future tasks in your (electronic) diary. If you have a meeting in 14 days' time about an important report you should put an entry in your diary 12 days from now to read the report. This will help you avoid running into trouble finding the time by the due date.
- Try to deal with new tasks as quickly as possible. The motto here is "Do it now". Writing the minutes of a meeting immediately after the conclusion of the meeting might cost you an hour, whereas after a week they might require two hours to write. Postponing activities usually costs extra time.
- Each day plan one or two tasks that can be finished that day. At the end of the day this will give you the feeling of having accomplished something.
- Do difficult things when you are fit. For most people this is in the morning. After a meal people are less capable of performing complex tasks.
- Keep your contacts with your colleagues short when you are busy.
- Make realistic appointments. Only agree to things you can manage, otherwise you will waste both your time and others'.
- Try to make as few mistakes as possible. Preventing a mistake might take five minutes; rectifying a mistake might take a day.
- Try to avoid problems. Resolving problems can be quite time-consuming.
- Be selective about the meetings you attend. You do not have to be in on everything. Some meetings might be a waste of time for you.
- Only read things that are useful. A lot of paperwork might find its way to your desk. Much of it is completely uninteresting and can be thrown out immediately. If so, do just that. If you do not throw them out you will have to deal with them in some way, if only to put them from one stack into another.
- Make sure of a clean working space. If you ask some people for a document they know exactly where to find it: somewhere in a stack half a meter high. Looking for things costs time. Important papers should be filed in clearly labelled and clearly arranged folders.
- E-mail could save you a lot of time trying to reach the other party. It can also waste time if you do not use it sensibly. Some people send copies of everything to everybody. You should make arrangements about what should be sent on and what should not.

- A cell phone is a very useful tool because you can be reached at all times. However, do you really want to be? You should give your cell number only to those people who are really allowed to call you at any time. This will probably be a limited number.
- Take time to relax, and be regular about this. Do not skip meals, no matter how busy you are. Take good care of your physical condition.
- Be positive in your dealings with other people. A negative atmosphere makes it difficult to get your coworkers to do anything for you. If a coworker has dealt with a situation poorly, a remark such as "You've made a mistake and you've got to fix it" will just put him into a bad mood. However, if you ask him to look over the solution critically, this will sound much more respectful and he will be more inclined to try and resolve the problem. Most people find it hard to take criticism.

If you have the opportunity to take a class on time management, this is absolutely worthwhile. The time that you put into it more than pays for itself in the long run.

4

4.12 Mini-course on MS Project on the website

You can download the "Mini-course on MS Project" as a PDF file from the website accompanying this book. This way you can teach yourself the most important functions of MS Project. Obviously this means you must own or have access to this program.

Assignments

4.1   What is the difference between a planning and a project plan?

4.2   "We do not have time for a schedule." Comment.

4.3   "The project manager will therefore have to assess the schedules the
            project's participants have drawn up on the basis of how realistic they
            seem". Explain.

4.4   What is meant by:
    a Milestones
    b Dependencies
    c A critical activity
    d A critical path
    e ASAP and ALAP
    f Resources
    g Slack in a plan
    h A Gantt chart
    i A network diagram
    j Duration
    k Time spent

4.5   Create a Work Breakdown Structure for:
    a An excursion
    b A staff day
    c The development and introduction of a new course

4.6   **a** A Gantt chart could suggest dependencies that do not exist. Explain.
    b What are you doing when you are drawing up a network diagram manually:
            planning the duration or the required working hours of a project? Explain.
    c Why should the number of dependencies be kept to a minimum?

4.7   **a** When drawing up a network diagram, what is the advantage of using
            planning software rather than doing it by hand?
    b What role do calendars play in planning software?

4.8   As the following indicates, there is a lot involved in cooking a meal. A man
            has to cook a meal for his friends. The meal has to be ready at 7 p.m. The
            shopping still has to be done. There are three courses: soup, main course,
            dessert. The main course consists of potatoes, vegetables and steak.
            A table of activities (Table 4.3) is shown hereafter.

TABLE 4.3 belonging to assignment 4.8

	Activity	Minutes	Only after:
A	Shopping	60	–
B	Make stock	60	A
C	Wash vegetables	3	A
D	Peel potatoes	7	A
E	Make soup	30	B, C
F	Boil vegetables	20	C
G	Boil potatoes	20	D
H	Grill meat	15	A
I	Make dessert	10	A
J	Eat soup	10	E
K	Eat main course	10	F, G, H, J
L	Eat dessert	5	I, K

a Make a network diagram based on this table of activities. Which of the activities are on the critical path?
b What is the duration of this "project"?
c Make a Gantt chart based on the network diagram.
d Because the potato peeler cannot be found, a new one has to be bought. This means that activity D lasts 90 minutes instead of 7 minutes. What will the duration be now? Use the network diagram.

4.9 A company wants to develop a new product. The plans have to include marketing (see Table 4.4.).

TABLE 4.4 belonging to assignment 4.9

	Activity	Time	Only after:
A	Develop the product	3	–
B	Cost analysis	2	A
C	Make prototype	3	A
D	Order material	4	A
E	Prepare sale actions	4	B, C
F	Prepare production line	2	C
G	Instruct factory staff	1	C
H	Production	8	B, D, F, G
I	Distribute to wholesalers	2	E, H
J	Distribute to retailers	2	I

	Activity	Time	Only after:
K	Announce sale	4	E
L	Sell	2	J, K

a Make a network diagram.
b What is the critical path?
c What is the duration of the project?
d Make a Gantt chart (indicate slack).

4.10 Look at the following table of activities (Table 4.5).

TABLE 4.5 belonging to assignment 4.10

	Activity	Days	After
A	Activity A	5	-
B	Activity B	7	-
C	Activity C	3	A
D	Activity D	5	A
E	Activity E	6	B, C
F	Activity F	3	D
G	Activity G	6	E, F
H	Activity H	9	B
I	Activity I	2	H, G

a Make a network diagram based on this table of activities.
b What activities are on the critical path?
c What is the duration of the project?
d Make a Gantt chart based on the network diagram.
e Which of the activities have slack? How much?

4.11 Choose one of the projects from section 1.2 and create a Work Breakdown Structure for its activities.

4.12 In this assignment you have to plan a project yourself. A number of projects have been mentioned in Section 1.2 of this book.
a Choose one of these projects or a project of your own. Discuss your choice of project with your teacher or trainer.
b Form a group of two to three people and together find approximately 30 activities for the chosen project. Remember those activities that are part of the preparation and those that need to take place after completion of the project. If necessary consult an expert in the field of your project.
c Create a well-organized plan by arranging the tasks in logical groups.
d Determine the dependencies between the activities. Try to keep the number as low as you can. If A must follow B and B must follow C, then A must

logically also follow C. Such a derived dependency is already covered by other dependencies and should not be included.
e After consultation with your teacher/trainer you should make:
- A manual network diagram
- A manual network diagram and a Gantt chart
- A Gantt chart using a computer program

4.13   Think of an activity that
a Should be done as soon as possible (ASAP)
b Should be done as late as possible (ALAP)
c Should be done on an exact date
d Should not be done before a certain date
e Should not be done after a certain date

4.14   Make a list of all the terms in section 4.9 and give a definition of each term.

4.15   Projects involve various resources – people, materials and tools. Give two examples of materials that can be used and two examples of tools.

4.16   Using a computer program, make a Gantt chart for the following:
a Assignment 4.9
b Assignment 4.10
c Assignment 4.12
d Assignment 4.8
e Your own thesis
f The remainder of your course of study
g Your summer vacation (including preparations)

4.17   Discuss the following statements in a group:
- A completely new project cannot be planned and attempting to do so is a waste of time.
- Time records for project workers is one big lie and therefore a waste of time.
- There is always only one critical path in a schedule.
- The critical path of a project is set in concrete and cannot be altered.
- If an activity is carried out ALAP it becomes part of the critical path.

4.18   To spend time efficiently, it is important to know "where all the time goes".
a Re-examine section 4.11 on Time Management.
b Estimate how many hours you need each week for all of your activities. This includes sleeping, eating, attending classes, studying at home, working and socializing.
c Describe five situations in which you are wasting time.
d Describe five situations in which you could improve your own productivity.
e Think about what you are going to be doing next week. Plan all activities in your diary. Do not forget to jot down any preparation work that is required. Also jot down on Monday of next the week that you need to draw up a new schedule for that week.
f Which five of the tips in section 4.11 are most useful for you?
g For one whole week, write down how you spend your time every day. You can do this for more than a week of course.
h Compare your estimate from point b with the actual numbers from point g. Do they match? If not, what is the reason?

This part of the book describes a number of practical tools and skills required to tackle projects, including how to draw up a project plan and write a report.

There is, however, no one way of going about any of the processes these chapters deal with. Meetings, for example, can be held in a number of different ways. The approach opted for in this part has been chosen specifically with projects in mind.

The skills dealt with in each chapter are described in more or less technical terms. In the chapter on conducting meetings, for instance, the processes essential for the smooth running of a meeting are dealt with. While conversation and discussion techniques are crucial aspects of these processes, they fall outside the scope of the book. You will need to consult other sources for training in these techniques.

The second half of this book can be considered a handbook for projects. Companies and organizations might find such a handbook useful for a variety of reasons:
- Project groups do not have to constantly reinvent the wheel.
- All project groups approach their projects in similar ways. Knowing these ways is a real advantage, as it makes it easier to manage the various results of the project.
- It is a tool for guaranteeing the quality of the project.
- It will encourage the company to adopt a uniform philosophy with regard to projects.

This part can be used in two ways:
1 As a checklist for activities that need to be carried out
2 As a mandatory set of guidelines

PART 2

Project tools

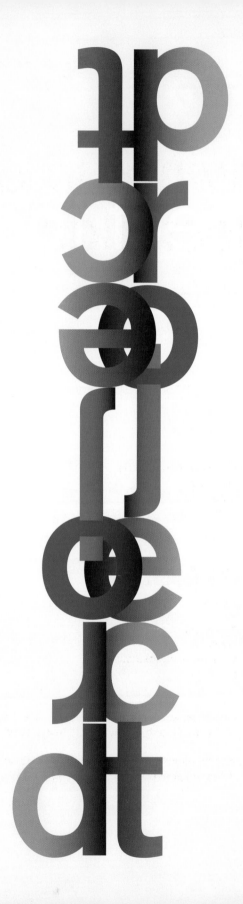

5
Drawing up a project plan

Right from the initial stages, working according to plan is an important aspect of a project. The project plan – a document that provides a detailed description of a project – plays a crucial role in this.
This chapter will describe a method for drawing up a project plan such that everyone knows what is expected of him or her and the sponsor obtains what he wants.

5.1 The project plan

Project plan

The project plan is usually drawn up by the project manager. He should only do so after the following have taken place:
- A number of **interviews** with the sponsor.
- Consultation and interviews with experts and all parties involved (the stakeholders).
- Collection and examination of documents that may be important for the project, such as descriptions of the organization, annual reports, reports from previous projects and the minutes of meetings.

The project plan must make the course of events clear to everyone: a project plan defines the project. It must be written in such a way that it is just as understandable for outsiders.

Plan of approach

A project plan is sometimes also called a *plan of approach*. A project plan should not be confused with a schedule. A schedule indicates who will do what and when. A schedule is merely one part of a project plan (it has been described in detail in Chapter 4).

If the project is a small one, a single project plan for the entire project will suffice.

 The website accompanying this book contains an MS Word model that can be downloaded for formulating a project plan.

5.2 Dividing the project plan into sections

As indicated above, a project plan is a document in which the entire project is defined. While the document should consist of a number of sections, how the contents are spread among the sections is a matter of choice. The important thing is that the plan be both clear and complete. All of the TMQIO factors described in section 3.9 must be included. It is convenient if everyone in a particular company draws up a project plan in the same way. A standard method for doing this is described in this chapter.

The project plan consists of a number of sections, which are listed in Table 5.1 and Figure 5.1.

TABLE 5.1 The project plan section by section

Section	Topic
1 Background information	Where (in what environment) is the project taking place?
2 The project result	Why are we carrying out this project and what is the desired final result?
3 Project activities	What do we need to do to achieve the project goal?
4 Project limits	What are the boundaries of the project?
5 The products	What are the intermediate products?
6 Quality control	How can we ensure the sufficient quality of all products?
7 The project organization	Who is participating and how do we plan to collaborate?
8 Schedule	Who is doing what when?
9 Costs and benefits	What will the project cost and what will it yield?
10 Risk analysis	What could cause the project to fail?

FIGURE 5.1 The project plan section by section

In sections 5.3 to 5.12, a method will be described for creating a suitable project plan. Each section forms the basis for a section of the project plan. The website accompanying this book includes a checklist that can be used to check a project plan for completeness.

5.3 Background information

The future members of the project team, the organization in which the project is being carried out, and the outside world will need background information about the project. One way of doing this is including the information – the "project environment" – in the project plan. The information should be such that even the uninitiated can form a picture of both the project and the organization in which the project is being carried out.

- Give your project a clear, preferably original, and **catchy** *name*! This makes it easier to remember within the organization. Examples of memorable names are Decibel (switch to 10-digit telephone numbers at KPN Telecom) and Operation Desert Storm (the first war between Iraq and the United States) and the North/South line (subway connection between Amsterdam North and Amsterdam South).

5

**Person
carrying out
the project**

- State the organization commissioning the project (i.e. the party that is paying for it) and the person who is acting as the **sponsor**. The sponsor must approve the final project plan. He or she will also want to evaluate the results at the end of the project.
- State the person or organization that is carrying out the project. Also state the person ultimately responsible for the completion of the project. This does not have to be written in detail since it is worked out in more detail in section 7 of the project plan, which covers project organization.
- Give a description of the organization in which the project is being carried out. What does the company do? What departments does it have? Who answers to whom? The best technique is to describe the background elements in order of decreasing size: for example, first the company, then the business unit, and finally the department (see Fig. 5.2.).
- Give an account of the project's history. Why is this project important? Is this project a continuation of another project? What were that project's outcomes? How does that project affect this one? How does this project relate to others still in the pipeline?
- Indicate the **stakeholders** of the project (see section 2.2), i.e. those with an interest in the final results of the project. Also state what kind of interest this is.
- Briefly describe how the sponsor will be approving the project plan.
- Give a short description of the layout of the various section of the project plan.

This information should be incorporated into "Background information", the first section of your project plan (see Figure 5.1).

FIGURE 5.2 Background elements in order of decrasing size

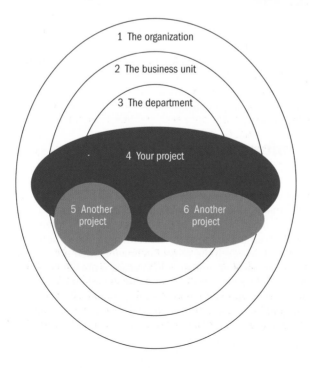

1 The organization

2 The business unit

3 The department

4 Your project

5 Another project

6 Another project

5.4 The project result

The second section of the project plan (see Figure 5.1) describes the ultimate project outcome based on the goals and commission. This section of the project plan explains why the project is being carried out. It also answers the following question: "What is the final result after the project is finished?" So this chapter defines the project result.

Project goal

The goal of the project expresses *why* the project is being carried out. What does the sponsor want to achieve by having this project carried out? Examples of goals are:

Project goal
Why

- Promote good health
- Offer a solution for an existing production problem
- Promote the integration of minorities
- Accelerate the production process for the company's products
- Socially responsible business practices, such as producing less waste or using less energy
- Make more profit
- Reduce hospital waiting lists
- Solve student housing problems
- Maintain market share (or increase it)

Project goals need to be formulated using the SMART principles. It is therefore advisable to reread section 1.12 on this concept. Incidentally, the goals stated in this section have not yet been formulated using the SMART principles.

Goals are often broken down into a number of sub-goals in a project plan.

Definition of the problem: research situations only

If your project does not entail research, you can skip the definition of the problem. However, if the project does involve research, not only do goals need to be defined, but also the *problem*. This is usually formulated in terms of a research question (Grit & Julsing, 2009). The research report that is written – based on the research conducted – provides an answer to the question formulated as the definition of the problem.

Problem

A few examples of a problem to be defined:

- What kinds of properties and prices must new product X have in order to achieve sales of two billion dollars per year? And how should the production of the new product be organized?
- What are the causes behind the waiting lists for heart surgery and what measures can be taken to cut these in half?

It will often be necessary to elaborate on the goals or problem, formulating them in terms of a number of sub-goals or sub-problems.

Project result description

The project result description is derived from the goal and states the desired outcome(s) of the project. It should therefore describe the *project result* – the end product of the project – in as much detail as possible. Make sure to consult with the sponsor about this; there should be no doubts about the end result or the project will fail before it has even begun! How, for example, can you draw up a good schedule if you do not know

What

End result

exactly what the project result should be? And how can you calculate the costs of a project if the details are not yet known? In other words, the project result description determines the success or failure of the project. It is also advisable to formulate the project result description as an imperative, such as "Investigate the..." or "Design a...". You can subdivide the description into various project results if desired. In addition to your own description, you can refer to the written commission as drawn up by the sponsor. If you have not or not yet received such a description, try to do so.

Program of requirements   If a *program of requirements* is established together with the sponsor, this can also be used to describe the project results.

Experience has shown that many people find it difficult to formulate goals and to write a project assignment and result description. The following four examples might therefore be helpful.

EXAMPLE 5.1

The exhibition

To achieve the goal of introducing a broader audience to abstract art, the following task description was developed: organize an overview exhibition in the Museum Booijmans van Beuningen in Rotterdam using works by Spanish artist Salvador Dalí from at least five different museums based on the following requirements:

- The exhibition must run from April I to December I, 2013.
- A minimum of 200 of this artist's works must be on display.

- At least 100,000 people must visit the exhibition.
- The net costs to the sponsor (difference between income and expenditure) must not exceed 10,000 euros.
- The project includes the acquisition and transport of the works of art.

As you can see, the use of figures makes the description of the project result much clearer and more precise. You can almost see the visitors walking through the halls of the museum!

EXAMPLE 5.2

Study into hospital waiting lists

The goal of the study is to cut the waiting lists at hospital X in half. The task description: write a research report with recommendations for reducing waiting lists at hospital X. The project must be completely finished by October 25, 2012. A budget of $25,000 has been provided.

The study must meet the following requirements:

a Units P, Q and R must be involved in the study.
b The following persons must be interviewed: ....
c ...

The final research report must contain the following sections:

a Description of the seriousness of the problem
b ...

The results of the study must also be presented to the board of directors. In other words, the final results of this project are a research report and a presentation. Effectively formulating the requirements listed above and the sections at the start of the project reduces the chance of the project group turning in a useless report.

EXAMPLE 5.3

Problems at a factory

A factory is experiencing problems with delivering its end products to its customers on time. The competition is doing much better. So the factory starts up a project to improve its delivery times. The SMART goal is to reduce the delivery time of the product from ten to four days. The Production Department and Transportation Department are together responsible for achieving this goal by the end of the calendar year. Two projects are started up in order to

achieve this goal. Project 1: Replace the five old brand X machines with faster brand Y machines and make sure they are in operation by November 1. Organize the production department so that the production time using the new machines is reduced from eight days to three days. Project 2: Make sure that the delivery time of the end product is reduced from two days to one day by December 1st.

EXAMPLE 5.4

A building project

Build a motor yacht that satisfies the specifications shown in the enclosed drawings and list of requirements. The yacht must be delivered by July 15, 2010 at the latest for a purchase price of 400,000 dollars.
Instead of a motor yacht, this could be a

house, building or bridge. The point is, the final product to be delivered is specified. If you are asked to write a project plan as part of a school assignment, you will need to be more specific than simply "build a hospital wing" or "build a logistics centre in the harbour".

5.5 Project activities

A project is likely to involve a number of activities. If you are carrying out a certain type of project for the first time, you are unlikely to be familiar with all of them. Do not hesitate to consult others who have carried out a similar project. It is also helpful to create a *Work Breakdown Structure* (see section 4.7). The following action points must be kept in mind when planning activities.

Work Breakdown Structure

- Try to identify the activities that have to be carried out as completely as possible. If you do not, you may find it impossible to draw up useful schedules and cost calculations properly.
- Include the **preliminary design** in the list of activities. By doing so, the overall costs of the project will be included in any subsequent calculation of costs. Look at the following hypothetical list:
  Drawing up a project plan (**group title**):
  – Collect and study the information.
  – Hold discussions with the sponsor and those with expert knowledge.
  – Make a provisional project plan.
  – Discuss the project plan with the sponsor.
  – Draw up the definitive project plan.

- Try to group the activities in a logical manner. Give each group of activities a group title. Grouping provides clarity and is useful when the schedules are being drawn up (also see example 5.5).
- When you are grouping the activities, *arrange them by* **level** *according to the amount of work* required. A level could be (from the top down): a phase, a group or an activity.
- At this point, you do not have to worry about when an activity should be carried out and by whom. Once the project members are lined up, you can detail this in your plan of approach (Section 8: "Schedule").

EXAMPLE 5.5

Grouping activities

The following production phase activities are not really comparable:
- Construct foundations
- Positioning the walls

- Excavate foundations
- Build foundation walls
- Lay the floor
- Seal the floor

After all, constructing foundations requires a great deal more time than positioning the walls. A more coherent grouping would be as follows:

Construction of foundations (group with the following activities):

Construction of walls (group with the following activities):
- Position the walls
- Build the interior walls
- Build the exterior walls
- Point up the exterior walls

It is not necessary to include the weekly project meetings in the section on project activities (Chapter 3). Such meetings are included in "The project organization", Section 7 of your project plan (see Figure 5.1).

5.6 Project limits

Scope

What falls within the project's scope and what does not is frequently unclear. Sometimes it seems clear, but it later turns out that sponsor and the project manager each had their own interpretation.

Boundaries of the project

In order to prevent unclear situations from developing, you should describe the *boundaries of the project*. In other words, you should *demarcate* it. Unclear demarcation constitutes a major threat to any project, and projects often fail on this point. After all, if it is unclear what is and what is not part of a project, then it is by definition impossible to draw up a proper schedule.

In defining the boundaries, ask yourself the following two important questions (also see Example 5.6 and Figure 5.3):

1 When does the project finish? (i.e. the "length" of the project) Does your new office building construction project simply involve construction of the new building or are you also responsible for the relocation? Although it is stretching the imagination, the length of the project might conceivably include the latter.

2 What does the project include? (i.e. the "width" of the project) If relocation is the project, is it simply relocation of your own department or all departments? Look at the following situation:

FIGURE 5.3 Project boundaries and milestones

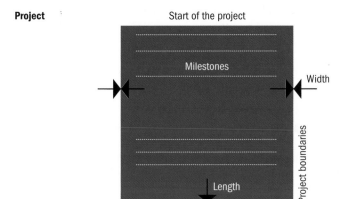

Everything that is carried out as part of the project is called the *"scope"* of the project. The word "scope" literally means size, range and domain.   **Scope**

EXAMPLE 5.6

Length and width of a project

You are involved in a project involving computerization of the financial administration. Do you only include the sales administration or does the purchasing administration also fall within your scope? This falls under the "width" of the project. Is training of the staff and installation of the software your responsibility? This falls under the "length" of your project.

As was suggested above, misunderstandings based on uncertainty about what is and what is not part of the project should be avoided at all costs. *Demarcate* the project clearly: **Demarcate**
- Determine whether those activities that could be considered "border-line" are part of the project.
- Indicate those borderline activities that do not fall within the project scope. It may seem strange to list activities that will not be done, but this makes it very clear for both the sponsor and the project manager.
- Indicate when the project will start as well as the repercussions of starting at a later date.
- Indicate the project's completion date.
- Indicate the maximum amount of the budget.
- Stipulate the preconditions that have to be met for the project to have a chance of success.

Preconditions   *Preconditions* are factors that the project group usually has little control over, but which must be satisfied in order to ensure a successful project. They serve as a "warning" to the sponsor: "Dear Sponsor, make sure that…. is taken care of or your project will fail." In other words, what does the sponsor need to do to make sure the project is a success? Examples of preconditions are: project members must be made available, another project must be finished first, the right tools must be made available or permission must be received from the municipality before construction can begin.

The results of these activities are then incorporated into Section 4, "Project limits", of your plan of approach (see Figure 5.1).

5.7 Intermediate results

Your project group will carry out a number of activities. These will result in all sorts of intermediate results or "products". In this context, the term "intermediate result" should be interpreted broadly: it need not refer to a physical object. An event such as the official opening of a building can also be an intermediate result. It is important to identify the result and to work towards it.

Project results   All results (intermediate and otherwise) together result in the *project results* desired by the sponsor. This is represented by the large circle shown in Figure 5.4.

FIGURE 5.4 All intermediate products together yield the ultimate project result

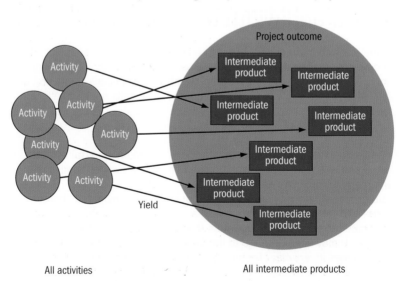

Project results are also described in section 2, "The project result", of the project plan.

EXAMPLE 5.7

Intermediate results of projects

The following are some examples of intermediate results of various types of projects:
- A report (final report, interim report)
- A construction drawing for a machine
- A bus arriving at a school in time for a school outing
- A mould for making plastic objects
- An installed machine (such as a lathe or computer)
- A computer program ready for operation
- A training plan
- Trained colleagues
- Reports of interviews
- A project plan
- A management summary
- The opening of a store
- A cost/benefit analysis
- A new production process that has been implemented

Since you are producing an intermediate result (product) and doing so to a deadline, the project's progress is *measurable*. You can regard an important intermediate result as a *milestone* in the schedule (also see Fig. 5.3). However, having too many milestones can distort the picture. You can include this in Section 5 of your project plan ("Intermediate results") (see Figure 5.1).

Measurable
Milestone

5.8 Quality control

The section on quality control in the project plan (Section 6) deals with the quality of the end product (and all intermediate products) referred to in the previous section. How can you guarantee their quality? Keep in mind that it is the sponsor who ultimately decides whether the quality of the end result (end product) of the project is sufficient. But how can you make sure this quality is sufficient? You can guarantee the quality in the following ways:
- Describe the desired *quality of the project result* (see section 2, "The project result", of the plan of approach). Also describe how the sponsor will assess this quality after the project has been completed.
- The sponsor will have to be reassured early on – during the project – about the *quality* of the project and project results. You can do this in advance in your project plan by determining how you plan to assess the quality of each of the intermediate results (from Section 5 on "Intermediate results") while carrying out the project.
- Indicate what **checks** will be carried out to guarantee the quality. These could include both test and technical procedures.
- Obtaining **feedback** on a project plan, a management summary, a report or an interview is a way of guaranteeing its quality.
- Request external advice. You could have a product or an intermediate result evaluated by an expert from outside your project team. For example, if your project requires you to draw up a questionnaire, it is advisable to have the questions assessed by a specialist in the field.
- Indicate the *standards and techniques* that apply to and are used within the organization. If these do not yet exist, establish the standards yourself. If necessary, consult other interested parties.
- Indicate the **tools and techniques** to be employed in making the diagrams and drawings.

Quality end product

Quality end results

5

- Indicate what software is used. You could, for example, specify the word processor, project planning software and other software. Make an effort to standardize the systems and thus make them more interconnectable.

Deviations
- If you *deviate* from the organization's commonly used standards, explain why.

Speed and quality are often conflicting goals. If you rush through an activity you may gain in terms of time but not quality. Delivering quality costs both time and money. There must be a balance between the quality that is delivered and the effort that this takes. Too high a standard of quality may cost too much. The layout of a report on an interview, for example, need not meet the same standards as the layout of an advertising brochure.

5.9 The project organization

A project falls outside of the normal business of an organization. You must make it clear to all parties involved what role they and others will play in the project plan and what the rules for personal interaction are (also see Chapter 2 of this book.).
Information is also essential for the organization of a project and is discussed in this section.

Organization
When drawing up a project plan, you need to find suitable project members, ones who have the right expertise and the right skills. Make sure you have a well-balanced team (see the Belbin roles in section 2.9). You will also have to negotiate with the sponsor and other relevant parties about using these people for your project. Since naturally you want only the best people for your project, you might meet some resistance.

The following positions could be considered:
- Project Manager
- Working Group Manager (if applicable)
- Project Secretary
- Project Team Member
- Adviser

Assign the positions and tasks to the various individuals. This should be done in consultation with the sponsor and the departmental heads.
- List the names, addresses, phone numbers and e-mail addresses of all project members.
- Indicate the required **availability** of the team members (full-time, 2 days a week, etc.). Vacations and other days off must be taken into consideration and set out clearly in agreements. This is particularly important: if the agreements are not lived up to, this will have direct repercussions on the completion date of your project.
- Link the positions to individuals.
- Establish what **authority** each project member holds and what his or her responsibilities are (also see Chapter 2, "People working on projects").
- Indicate how and to whom you will **report** (i.e. to whom you are accountable). This may, for example, be the steering committee, the board of directors or the departmental heads.

5

- With larger projects, it may be necessary to receive secretarial support or even set up a complete **project office** for administrative matters such as keeping files, the financial administration, recording the hours worked, and correspondence (also see section 5.14.)

Information
Make sure that all interested parties (stakeholders) are well informed throughout the project. The nature of the information is highly diverse and includes information:
- Relevant to the project members
- Relevant to the sponsor, steering committee (if any) and departmental managers involved in the project
- Relevant to the user of the end product of the project
- Relevant to anyone who is "inconvenienced" by the project

If the project is complex, you can carry out a *stakeholder analysis* in which you indicate who is involved and who has an interest in the project for every stakeholder. A "Stakeholder analysis checklist" can be downloaded from the website. The stakeholder analysis can be used to determine who should produce which information and who should receive which information. This can be displayed in a *information matrix*. The "Sample information matrix" can be downloaded from the website.

Stakeholder analysis

Information matrix

There might be a considerable amount of resistance to the project. That is because projects often result in change and not everyone is comfortable with change. A mega project involving the construction of a new railway line or freeway section can expect considerable resistance from environmental groups and neighbouring residents. But projects that also result in major change within organizations will not always be considered positive. That is why those working on projects involving reorganization, the implementation of new working methods or the automation of work processes should always expect some degree of resistance. Before a project is started up, arrangements should be made to "sell" the project to the outside world.

Large projects have members who take care of the *public relations* (PR) aspect of the project. They are responsible for "selling" the project to the stakeholders (all those involved) and sometimes writing a complete *communication plan* based on the stakeholder analysis. It is a good idea to review your list of project activities (Section 3 of your plan of approach) to make sure you have taken this problem sufficiently into consideration.

Public relations

Communication plan

Coordination
Effective collaboration depends on good *coordination* of the activities. This applies both to the project activities as well as the activities involving the outside environment. The following tips will help you coordinate the project effectively:
- Establish how often and when you are going to hold **meetings** with the project team, the steering committee and the sponsor. Who will receive an agenda and the minutes?
- Together with the sponsor, establish how the project's members should *record* their *time*. Usually this will be via a weekly record of the hours worked (also see section 3.10, "Monitoring the progress"). A "Time registration form" can be downloaded from the website to use as

Coordination

Record time

reference. In an organization where project-based work practices are common, the time records can usually be done by computer. The participants enter their hours worked under the project in question directly from their workstations. Calculations are done on the basis of each participant's hourly rate and financial information relating to the time spent on a project is then readily available.

- Indicate whether you want a written **weekly report** from the members of the project team. A weekly report will contain a description of what was done the previous week. The activities that are planned for the following week may also be included in the weekly report.
- If you wish to maintain communication between members of the project team and others by **e-mail**, clear agreements must be made about how this should be done. It may include reading one's e-mail at least once a day.
- Set up a **filing system** for the project (see section 5.14).
- Establish which **virtual tools** (see section 2.10) you plan to use for collaborating within your project group.

All these matters fall under project organization and should be incorporated into section 7 ("The project organization") of your project plan (see Figure 5.1).

5.10 Schedule

Once you know what the project's activities are, what products are involved, what the project's milestones will be, and who is part of the project's team, you can start drawing up the schedules. A schedule provides an overview of activities in relation to time. A schedule also indicates which members of the project team have been assigned to various activities. A schedule enables you to estimate how long a project is going to take and how much it will cost. For more detailed information on the drawing up of schedules, see Chapter 4 in this book.

Drawing up a schedule
The following approach may be applied to *drawing up a schedule*:
- Transfer the activities listed in section 5.5 to an activities table (see Table 4.1).
- Include the duration and possibly also the required working time per activity in the table.
- Indicate what dependencies there are between the activities.
- Draw a network diagram if necessary.
- Draw a Gantt chart.

If available, consider using computer planning software.

 To draw up a schedule using the MS Project program, you can download the "Mini-course on MS Project" from the website www.projectmanagement-english.noordhoff.nl. The "Planning" spreadsheet model can be downloaded to simplify making a Gantt chart.

For more detailed information on drawing up a schedule, see Chapter 4 of this book.

5.11 Costs and benefits

Carrying out a project always takes time, and therefore costs money. It also involves use of other resources (for example, building materials), and has to produce something: the yield or benefits. It is up to the sponsor to weigh up the costs against the benefits and decide whether or not the project should be carried out. If the benefits are no greater than the costs, you should seriously consider not undertaking the project (see Fig. 5.5).

FIGURE 5.5 More benefits than costs

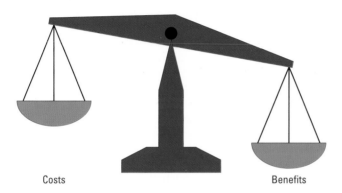

Costs   Benefits

A project is likely to involve the following costs:
- **Man-hours** (required working time). These hours can be converted into money by multiplying them by the hourly rates. Do not forget to include the time required to manage the project.
- **Other resources**. These could include the cost of materials, housing, acquisition of equipment, hiring technical aids and printing costs.
- **Exploitation costs**. These are costs incurred after the project has been completed. Exploitation costs do not necessarily have to be mentioned in the project plan. If, for example, the project outcome is a building, knowing the cost of the building will suffice. What the sponsor will be doing during the usage – exploitation – of the building is irrelevant to the building project. If necessary, consult with the sponsor about whether or not he wants a calculation of exploitation costs included in the project plan.

Unexpected expenditure may be included in the budget as an additional cost. This could, for example, be 10% of the overall costs. This will have to be negotiated with the sponsor. When you are calculating the costs you might have to assume some things. Make sure that these assumptions are clear to the sponsor and show how the calculation was made. **Unexpected expenditure**

The project's *benefits* could include the following: **Benefits**
- Immediate cost savings. Savings on the costs of personnel and materials after the project is completed.
- Additional income.
- Improved product quality. This can be translated into financial terms by estimating how much more of the product is likely to be sold.

- Better customer service. This may also result in increased sales.
- More highly motivated personnel. This may result in an improved product and less waste.
- In the case of a technical project such as the building of a ship, the benefits will consist of the sales price of the project outcomes, in this case the ship.

For the benefits as well, it should be indicated how the calculations were carried out and what assumptions were made. It is sometimes difficult to translate benefits into money. In consultation with the sponsor, you could decide to provide a brief summary of the costs and benefits. This should be stated in the Section 9 of your project plan, "Costs and benefits" (see Figure 5.1). You can also work out the costs and benefits using a spreadsheet program like MS Excel.

5.12 Risk analysis

A project's success might come under threat from all directions. Re-read sections 3.11 and 3.12 on risk analyses when formulating this section of your project plan. You will also find a step-by-step plan for carrying out a risk analysis as well as a categorization of risks.

Internal risks

Risks can be broken down into two types: internal and external. The *internal risks* may include the following:
- The project is not feasible. Sometimes the project's objectives simply cannot be attained within the prescribed time period and with the resources available.
- The duration is too long (more than two years, for example).
- The deadline is too fixed.
- There are too many areas of expertise involved.
- There is too little experience in working in a project-based way.
- The members of the project team are not used to scheduling.
- There is insufficient knowledge or expertise on the part of the members of the project team.
- The members of the project team are not sufficiently motivated.
- There is insufficient participation by the end users in the sponsor's organization.
- The project manager is unsuitable.
- The members of the project team who have to travel long distances to attend the meetings.
- There is insufficient familiarity with the project within the organization. Project team members function better if they know that other employees in the organization are watching them.
- The members of the project team who are unwilling or unable to work together.

External risks

The *external risks* may include the following:
- Insufficient time for reaching decisions.
- Too much dependence on the results of other projects. If a project involving the installation of sewers is not completed by the municipality in time, the contractor will be unable to start a project involving the building of a residential area.

- Insufficient cooperation by employees of the organization. In the case of reorganization projects, if the organization is set against the changes, it may turn out to be impossible to complete the project successfully.
- The project's scope has not been clearly defined.
- A lack of ongoing preparedness on the part of the departments to supply employees for the project team. If the project has run for some time, department heads will often try to recall employees that have been detached. Sometimes this is attempted by undermining the project.
- Changes to the composition of the project team.
- A goal that differs from the goal as formulated in the project plan. Sometimes the parties involved – including the sponsor – have ulterior motives in relation to the project that are in conflict with the project's formal goal.

You should indicate in Section 7 of your project plan what risks threaten the project and how serious they are. There are techniques for rating the degree of risk based on ranking them. This is illustrated in Appendix 1. The value of such a calculated degree of risk is, however, a matter for debate. Companies and projects may also vary in the type of analysis they employ. If the sponsor requests such a quantitative risk analysis, you could use the method in Appendix 1 as a basis.

You can also download 1 *spreadsheet model* from the website, which can be used to perform the risk analysis in MS Excel.

5.13 Drawing up the project plan

If you have carried out the steps shown in sections 5.3 to 5.12, all the sections of your project plan will now be ready. Even if the sponsor considers a particular section to be unimportant, you should still include it in the table of contents, but with the following text in place of the text of that particular section: "In consultation with the sponsor, it has been decided that there will be no text in this section."

Your next step is to create a *cover page* and table of contents.   **Cover page**
The cover page should contain the following information:
- The text: "Project plan"
- As the title, the name of your project
- A subtitle (optional)
- The names of the organization and the sponsor
- The place and date of completion of the project plan
- The name of the project manager
- The names of the members of the project team and their e-mail addresses

After numbering the pages, you should compile a *table of contents*. The   **Table of**
best way to do this is automatically using a word processing program. You   **contents**
can then use the checklist at the back of this book to check to make sure you have not forgotten anything. Your draft (provisional) project plan is now finished.

You can now submit the provisional project plan to the sponsor. You should   **Discuss the**
also make an appointment to *discuss the plan*.   **plan**

In summary, you draw up a project plan as follows:
- Consult with all persons involved (including the sponsor, subject experts and future project members)
- Study any available documents that are important for the project
- Write a project plan
- Check the completeness of the plan using the checklist at the back of this book
- Submit the provisional project plan to the sponsor
- Discuss the provisional project plan
- Write the definitive project plan
- Submit the definitive project plan
- Wait for the final approval of the sponsor

Do not waste time and effort endlessly polishing up every aspect of your project plan. A project plan is a means of giving shape to your project: it is not an end in itself!

5.14 The project's files

It is very important that all project documents be stored carefully. A good filing system should be set up. It must be possible to quickly retrieve any document from the filing system. It is a good idea to select a member of the project team who has a feeling for filing as the *filing secretary*. Some people are absolutely unsuited to this sort of work! A glance at their desk is often sufficient to establish this. Sometimes the task is done by the project office.

Filing secretary

File

A *file* is a collection of folders in which information is stored. The best strategy is to create two different sets of files in your filing system:
1 Day-to-day files
2 Document files

Filing cabinets

It is also advisable to keep these files separate from each other and to store the documents in different folders or filing cabinets.

Log book

All matters that concern the organization and management of the project should go in the *day-to-day files.* The documents in this file are temporary by nature and most of them will be designed for accounting purposes (time records, progress accounts). In this sense, the file constitutes a kind of *log book.* When the project has been completed, the value of this file will rapidly diminish. The day-to-day files will contain documents such as:
- The provisional project plan
- Notes
- The commission
- The schedules (including any adjusted schedules)
- Progress reports and the project members' time records
- Agendas and minutes of various meetings
- Incoming and outgoing correspondence
- Memoranda

Document files

The *document files* should contain all of the project's documents: anything relating directly to the objects and the desired outcomes. The documents in

this file are likely to remain quite valuable even after the completion of the project. They will include such documents as the following:
- Reports of interviews
- Preliminary reports and the like
- Recommendations relating to the project itself
- Designs, diagrams, reports and the like created during the course of the project.

5.15 Other project management methods

The method described in this chapter for writing a project plan includes practical tools and skills for tackling projects. Since projects often fail, a number of different methods have also been devised for managing projects. A few examples are Prompt, Prince 11, Prodigy and Probaat. Some companies develop their own project approach. There are also methods that are used specifically in a particular field. ISD, ISAC, SDW and NIAM, for example, are often used in the field of automation. In a nutshell, there are various project management methods and techniques to choose from.

The *Prince II* project management method was developed by the British government. It is intended to make sure that the sponsor of larger projects gets the end product he or she expects. "Prince" stands for PRojects IN Controlled Environments.

Prince II

Prince II divides a project into phases. The original project goal is reviewed after every phase and decisions are then made as to the further carrying out of the project. The Prince method entails the use of a large number of checklists and guidelines for monitoring the completeness and quality of the project. One of the most important documents in Prince II is the formulation of the *Project Initiation Document*, or PID for short. This is a type of project plan that determines the approach, manner of progress reporting, establishment of responsibilities, products to be delivered, scheduling, risk factors, manner of acceptance and invoicing schedule. Other standard documents within this method include a request for change form.

Project Initiation Document

If all documents (templates) are used, the administrative burden (paper pile) can become quite large. With smaller projects, the choice can be made to use only some of the templates provided by Prince. When using Prince, all those involved in the project must be trained on using this methodology (by taking a course, for example).

As can be expected, a number of the elements found in Prince can also be found in the project plan described earlier in this chapter.

Assignments

5.1 In which phase of a project is the project plan drawn up?

5.2 What kinds of steps must a project manager take in order to write an acceptable project plan?

5.3
  a Why is it important to delineate the project's scope and preconditions in the project plan?
  b Explain (by means of an example) what is meant by the "length" of a project.
  c Do the same for the "width".
  d What are project milestones?
  e Why is it important not to set the project's quality standards too high?

5.4 "Projects have to produce products."
  a Explain why this is advisable.
  b Identify some "products" that a project involving organizing a school outing could produce.

5.5 List four job positions that a project team might require.

5.6 Indicate how each of the management aspects of Time, Money, Quality, Information and Organization (see Chapter 3) should be dealt with in the project plan.

5.7 A course of training or study also has a number of milestones. List some of them.

5.8
  a Explain what the difference is between the project's day-to-day files and the document files.
  b Indicate how useful each is likely to be after the completion of the project

5.9 Consider the following projects:
  1 An art exhibition
  2 The construction of a new hospital wing
  3 A computerization project
  4 An ISO-9000 quality control project
  5 The introduction of performance assessment talks
  6 A final thesis project
  7 A project you suggest yourself

Answer the following questions for each of the above projects:
a Identify some of the likely activities.
b Identify some of the project's likely boundaries.
c Name a number of likely intermediate products.
d List some of the likely costs and benefits.
e Mention some of the likely risks (threats).

5.10 Write a description (specifications) of the project result for each of the following projects. You will probably have to make up some details, though try not to let this stand in the way of defining the project as precisely as possible.
a The construction of a new warehouse
b The development of an Internet site for a company
c A computerization project
d An ISO-9000-quality control project
e Incorporating performance assessment discussions into the organization's human resource management

5.11 This assignment requires you to create a project plan for a project.
- Get together a project team of 2 or 3 persons.
- Section 1.2 of this book lists a number of projects. Select one of these projects. You could also take a project of your own. Discuss your choice with your trainer or teacher.
- The project plan should be as realistic as possible. If necessary, interview people who are experts in the area of your project. Alternatively, make up some details, but try and make them as realistic as you can.
- Write the project plan according to the guidelines given in this chapter. Write the plan in your capacity as the project manager. If the project is completely fictitious, think carefully about who the sponsor is.
- In consultation with your trainer, draw up a schedule (either manually or using planning software).
- Check your own provisional project plan against the "Project plan checklist", which can be downloaded from the website accompanying this book.
- Swap your project plan for that of another project team. Both teams should then read and evaluate each other's project plan. Use the same checklist for this purpose. Provide the other team with written feedback.
- Discuss the feedback on your own project plan with your team and incorporate it into your definitive project plan.
- In addition to the names of the members of your own project team, you should list the names of those members of the project team who gave the feedback ("Feedback from......"). This makes both project teams responsible for the project plan.
- Submit your project plan to your trainer or teacher for evaluation.

5.12 Form a group and discuss the following statements:
a Creating a project plan takes up a lot of time and is unnecessary if the project is small.
b A project manager should not accept any modifications to the project plan during the course of the project.
c The project plan must be amended if changes occur during the project.
d The project plan should preferably be drawn up by the sponsor.
e In some projects, a vague project plan may serve the sponsor's own interests.

© Noordhoff Uitgevers bv

5.13 The following project commissions are invalid because the results cannot be assessed. Indicate how they could be improved.

a Optimize the flow of goods within the company.

b Reduce the number of errors in allocating student loans.

c Computerize the production system.

d Improve the municipal services.

e Organize a study trip.

project

6

Carrying out a project

This chapter brings together all of the other chapters of this book. It describes how exactly you set to work carrying out a project from start to finish in an easy step-by-step manner. It also contains a practical mixture of the phases (Figure 1.3) and descriptive Chapter 3 "The project from start to finish".

⬛ 6.1 Step-by-step plan for project execution

The left side of Figure 6.1 shows the logical phases of a project: initiative, definition, design, preparation, execution and aftercare. These phases can be translated into four steps (the four blocks in the middle) that make up project execution. The "products" of each step are shown on the right of the figure.

FIGURE 6.1 How to do a project

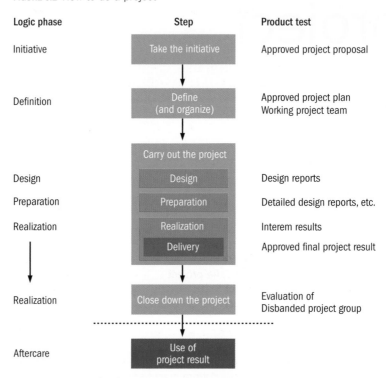

Logic phase	Step	Product test
Initiative	Take the initiative	Approved project proposal
Definition	Define (and organize)	Approved project plan / Working project team
	Carry out the project	
Design	Design	Design reports
Preparation	Preparation	Detailed design reports, etc.
Realization	Realization	Interem results
	Delivery	Approved final project result
Realization	Close down the project	Evaluation of / Disbanded project group
Aftercare	Use of project result	

The following sections describe each of the four steps in detail. Each step is broken down into activities and, for some activities, reference is made (in brackets) to important information found elsewhere in this book. Considerable reference is also made to the website accompanying this book with regard to useful resources that can be downloaded.

This chapter can be used as a helpful tool for both small and considerably large projects. Depending on the size of the project and sponsor requirements, you can skip or add activities as needed.

⬛ 6.2 Step 1: Take the initiative for the project

Initiative

A project does not just happen by itself: someone comes up with an idea and takes the *initiative* to start up a project. Someone has an interest in the results of the project. By the end of Step 1, it is clear who the sponsors of the project are and who the client is. A project proposal is also available, on which the decision is made as to whether or not to go through with the project. A project manager may also be designated during this phase, although this can also be done in the next step.

The first step entails the following:
- Exploring the topic.
- Formulating a project proposal (optional).
- Deciding whether or not to start the project.

These activities can be broken down into sub-activities, which are discussed below.

Exploring the topic
There is a reason to carry out a project. Someone has taken the initiative to start the project. The first step is to explore the topic.
1   Re-read the first three chapters of this book carefully.
2   Organize a meeting with the most important stakeholders (see Chapter 7 and the "Model **Agenda**" and the "Model **Minutes** on the website).
3   Determine the initiator of the project, such as a manager, regular staff member, future user or adviser.
4   Determine the reason for the project, such as serious failures within the organisation, an external threat, new opportunities or "something big" needs to be organized.
5   Determine what needs to take place in response to this need. For example:
    a Do nothing. Everything stays the same and no project is started.
    b The need is met "from within". In other words, the normal management of the organization takes the necessary measures and no project is started.
    c A project is started immediately. It is already clear that this project is necessary but, to save time, a project plan is written instead of a project proposal. Continue with Step 2.
    d Formulate a project proposal. That's the document on which the decision is made as to whether or not to go through with the project.
6   Form ideas about the goal of the project and the **project result** to be achieved. These will be worked out in more detail in Step 2 in the project proposal and project plan.
7   Determine the **sponsors**, if any, and look into a possible budget for the project.
8   Determine the official **client** (section 2.3).
9   Determine a possible **project manager** (section 2.5).
10 If relevant, set up a steering committee (section 2.15).

Formulate a project proposal
A *project proposal* is a go/no-go document. This means that the decision whether or not to go through with the project is based on this document. The proposal is written by the sponsor, initiator or candidate project manager.   **Project proposal**

If the project concerns a study, the project proposal is usually called a *research proposal*. By way of comparison, students of higher education are   **Research proposal** often required to write a thesis proposal in order to obtain approval for their thesis project.

1   Decide who is going to write the project proposal. If this is not the sponsor, one or more meetings will have to be scheduled between the sponsor and the person writing the project proposal. See the "**Initial interview** checklist" on the website.

2   Compile the information needed to write the project proposal (section 3.2).
3   Determine the feasibility of the project.

4   Write the project proposal. See "Model **Project proposal**" on the website.

Decide whether or not to start the project

The project proposal is evaluated by the sponsors and client and the decision is made whether or not to go through with the project. This process entails the following activities:

1   Discuss the project proposal with the important **stakeholders**, such as the sponsor and management.
2   Brainstorm on the composition of the project group, i.e. the project manager and project members.
3   Find a suitable project manager and capable project members.
4   Make sure a decision is made on the project proposal. The proposal may be rejected, require revision or be approved.
5   Decide whether to outsource the project or carry it out internally. If the proposal is rejected, it may be possible to have the need met internally through taking measures.
6   Inform the stakeholders of the decision.

6.3 Step 2: Define and organise the project

Project plan

During Step 1, a decision is made as to whether or not to start the project. The next step is to write up a detailed *project plan*. If a project proposal has been written, it is used to formulate the plan of approach.

Note: the activities are grouped in logical order for this step. This does not mean that they need to be carried out in the same exact order as described here. The activities may very well be carried out simultaneously, as long as the project is defined in the form of an approved project plan by the end of Step 2. The project must also be organized and the project group ready to set to work carrying out the project.

The second step entails the following activities:
• Preparing the project plan.
• Writing the project plan.
• Approving the project plan.
• Organizing the project.

Preparing the project plan

The project plan is the definition of the project. It is a contract between the project group (by way of the project manager) and the sponsor. The project plan is described in detail in Chapter 5. Below is a list of activities to be carried out in writing the project plan. You will probably not carry out these

activities in the same order as described here and some activities may need to be carried out more than once. But the ultimate result will be an approved project plan. The "Model **project plan**" can be downloaded from the website as reference.
1   Carefully read through not only Chapter 3, but absolutely Chapter 5!
2   Inquire into the organization where the project will be carried out. Get to know its people and culture.
3   Hold one or more meetings/interviews with the sponsor (section 3.3). See the "**Initial interview** checklist" on the website.
4   Determine the end result of the project in as much detail as possible.
5   Brainstorm on possible project members.
6   Map out the stakeholders in detail.
7   Interview important stakeholders. Who are they? What advantage, disadvantage or other interest does each have in the project? How can they influence the project (section 2.2)?
8   If relevant, carry out a stakeholder analysis. See the "**Stakeholder analysis** checklist" on the website.
9   Obtain support and authority from the stakeholders.
10   Inquire into a financial budget among possible sponsors. In some cases, the budget may not consist of money, but of the efforts of employees (also considered a budget).
11   Negotiate on the budget for the project (section 2.13).
12   Obtain secretarial support if necessary.
13   Decide whether or not to divide up the project.
     a Determine whether the project is so large that is must be divided into several sub-projects.
     b Determine whether and how the project should be phased (for an explanation, see section 1.7 on phases).
     c Decide whether or not to start a pilot project (section 3.1).
     d Determine the decision-making issues and moments of the project (section 2.13).
14   Organize the time compensation for project members and replacements for the work currently carried out by these project members.

Write a project plan
When writing a project plan, good contact and coordination with the client is essential. Chapter 5 describes the layout and contents of the project plan.
1   Determine in detail the desired project result. This is the most important part of the entire project since it specifies – in as much detail as possible – what the project group is going to achieve (section 5.4).
2   Determine the goal of the project (section 5.4).
3   To prevent confusion, draw up a list of definitions to be used.
4   Determine the project activities to be carried out. Group them logically or in phases (section 5.5).
5   Find suitable project members and allocate tasks.
6   Determine the availability of project members and other involved parties.
7   Draw up a schedule (Chapter 4). If possible, use a professional planning program or the "Model **Schedule**" of the "Mini-course on MS Project" from the website.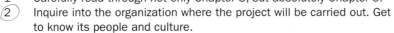
     a Determine the time to be spent on each activity.
     b Determine the interdependency of activities (order).

  c Determine the turnaround time based on the availability of project members.
  d Draw up a draft schedule.
  e Link project members to activities.
  f Discuss the planning.
  g Draw up a schedule.

8 Carry out a **risk analysis** (section 3.12). This can be done in a separate meeting, provided it is done thoroughly.

9 Calculate the costs and – if the client feels it is relevant – the profits.

10 Determine the end date of the project.

11 Determine who will supply which information during the project and who will receive that information. You can use the stakeholder analysis and incorporate it into an information matrix for this. See the "Model **information matrix**" on the website.

12 Describe the organization of the project.

13 Come up with a name for the project.

14 Write the (draft) project plan according to the instructions given in Chapter 5.

15 Check to make sure the project plan is complete. See the "**Completeness of project plan** checklist" on the website.

16 If it concerns a commercial project, you can formulate a **project quote**. See the explanation on "Formulating a project quote" on the website.

Have the project plan approved

Once the project plan is written, it must be discussed with the sponsor and ultimately approved.

1 Discuss the project plan with the sponsor.

2 Make clear-cut agreements on how to deal with changes to the project plan.

3 Inform the stakeholders of the project plan.

4 Present the project plan to the stakeholders. You can use the "**Presentation** checklist" in the website for this.

5 Write the final project plan based on comments on the draft.

6 Make sure the sponsor formally approves the project plan and makes a go/no-go decision.

Organize the project

The decision has been made to start the project and the project plan approved. The project group can now set to work (section 3.4).

1 Make meeting agreements within the project group, with the sponsor and, if relevant, the steering committee (section 2.14). Make sure the meetings are conducted professionally (see Chapter 7 and the "Model **Agenda**" and "Model **Minutes**" on the website).

2 Make team agreements (section 2.11).

3 Re-read Chapter 3 of this book.

4 Discuss the project plan, including the schedule, within the project group and with other relevant parties.

5 Organize the time registration of project members. See the "Model **Time registration** on the website.

6 Allocate tasks among the project members.

7 Make agreements on the resources to be used. If possible, use software as much as possible (section 2.10) and make sure there are good back-ups of all files. If relevant, use the "Model **Weekly report**" from the website.

8   Decide on collaborative tools to use, such as Windows Live, Google documents and convenient online software.
9   If relevant, draw up a communication plan for project stakeholders.
10   Consult regarding how reporting is to take place to the sponsor (see the "Model **Project progress report**" on the website).
11   Organize a project start-up meeting (section 3.5).

6.4 Step 3: Carry out the project

Once the project has been started, it is important to make sure the project yields the desired results within the available budget and at the agreed time. The third step entails the following activities:
- Carrying out the project in phases, if relevant.
- Managing information.
- Monitoring the time.
- Monitoring the quality of the project result.
- Ensuring good project organization.
- Monitoring the budget.
- Achieving the desired project result.

Carrying out the project in phases
Larger projects can be divided into *phases* during Step 3: "design", "preparation" (section 3.6) and "execution" (section 3.7). If this is to be done, it should have already been indicated in the project plan formulated as part of Step 2. At the end of each phase – with the exception of the last phase of course – a *phase transition* takes place to the next phase. When starting a subsequent phase, a variety of activities must be carried out, as described below.

Managing the information
To ensure a successful project, the parties involved must be well informed at all times. You must therefore make sure there is good internal communication within the project, such as by taking minutes and providing revised schedules.
1   Maintain good communication with the sponsor. You can do so using the "Model **Project progress report**" found on the website. If important information must be provided, you can send an official letter (see "**Writing letters**" on the website).
2   Maintain good communication with the project environment (section 2.2).
3   Maintain good archiving habits (section 5.14).

Monitoring the time
To make sure the project deadline is met, the schedule must be monitored at all times.
1   Check whether scheduled activities are finished on time and/or produce the desired results.
2   Keep track of the time registration sheets of all project members.
3   Update the schedule periodically, such as on every Monday.
4   Inform all involved parties of the revised schedule.

Monitoring the quality of the project result

All intermediate results ultimately yield the project result (Figure 5.4). Unfortunately, interim changes to the project cannot always be avoided.

1 Make sure the right materials, resources, services and people are purchased or brought in.
2 Monitor the **quality** of the resources used: methods and standards should be described in the project plan.
3 Monitor the quality of the intermediate results. During the project, various intermediate products will be produced, such as "semi-finished products", designs, reports and minutes. If the quality of these items is good, this will increase the likelihood of a high-quality end product (section 5.7).
4 Monitor the quality of the working method of the project members.
5 Determine what action should be taken with the **change requests** to the original project plan, such as by carrying out the following steps:
   a Determine the reason for the change.
   b Describe the desired change.
   c Determine the consequences of the change.
   d Calculate the costs of the change.
   e Determine the priority of the change.
   f Together with the sponsor, decide whether or not to grant the change request and incorporate the consequences into the schedule and cost calculation.

Ensuring good project organization

Making sure that project members work together effectively towards achieving the ultimate project result requires good organization.

1 Take measures that lead to good collaboration among project members.
2 Schedule regular meetings with the project group, such as weekly.
3 Schedule regular meetings with the sponsor, such as every other week or monthly.
4 Involve the **end users** of the project result in the project.
5 Compile information, such as time registration forms and information on deadlines met for scheduling purposes.
6 Check weekly whether the project members are still working as many hours on the project as promised.
7 Ensure a good **decision-making process** (section 2.13) within the project group.
8 Maintain contact with the important stakeholders. Deal appropriately with any resistance that could threaten the project.

Monitoring the budget (money)

To prevent the project from becoming more expensive than intended, the finances (incomes and expenditures) must be monitored closely.

1 Keep close track of all financial data, such as hours spent and goods and services purchased.
2 Calculate the **costs** of changes resulting from approved change requests.
3 Calculate the financial consequences of changes to the schedule.
4 Monitor the financial expenditure schedule.
5 Check often whether the financial profits (if relevant) still apply.

A phase transition?

If, earlier in this step (and in your project plan) you divided up the execution of the project into phases (such as the design, preparation and execution phases), you will have to carry out the following activities at the end of each phase:

1 Evaluate the schedule. What went well and what went wrong? Why? How can changes to the **planning and schedule** be avoided?
2 Calculate costs incurred and compare them to the original budget.
3 Evaluate the quality of the results of the previous phase.
4 Evaluate the above within the project and then discuss it with the sponsor.
5 Make the necessary decisions on what takes place next, such as a transition to another phase, ending the project prematurely (section 3.12) or providing the project result (below).

Repeat these activities until you are able to produce the product result.

Delivering the project result

The project is intended to produce a certain end result. The project result should be achieved by the end of Step 3.

1 Test out or check the project result within the project group.
2 Have the project result tested or checked by the sponsor and any other relevant parties, such as the future users of the project result.
3 Deliver the project result.
4 Present the project result to all parties involved (see Chapter 10 of this book and the "**Presentation** checklist" on the website).
5 Have the sponsor officially accept the project result.

6.5 Step 4: Conclude the project

Once the project has been completed and the project result delivered, a number of matters still need to be dealt with (section 3.8) and the project must be officially concluded.

Concluded

1 Make sure the project result can be maintained after delivery, such as by providing good descriptions or instructions for maintenance.
2 Make agreements for afterwards during the "use" of the project result, such as how the users will be supported or how changes can be made.
3 Settle the financial aspects of the project: pay any remaining invoices and carry out a subsequent financial calculation.
4 Evaluate the project result. This can be done using the project archive (section 5.14).
5 Evaluate project execution The **project archive** can also be used for this (section 5.14).
6 Together with the sponsor, draw up a **management summary** if desired (see Chapter 11).
7 Archive all **project documents** in an accessible manner.
8 Prepare the return of the project members to the organization.
9 If relevant, celebrate the completion of the project in a festive manner.
10 Formally dismantle the project group.

Assignments

6.1   Work out the step-by-step plan provided in this chapter for the following
projects:
   a The organization of a five-day excursion abroad
   b A large party for alumni (former students) at a college
   c A project that must be carried out by a sponsor

6.2   What would a project be divided into phases?

7
Organizing meetings

Working on projects usually involves quite a lot of meetings. This includes the project start-up meeting, consultations with the sponsor and weekly project group meetings. During these meetings the project manager or sponsor are likely to chair the meeting.

This chapter discusses the various aspects of a project meeting.

⬤7.1 Project meeting

A meeting is an organized occasion on which a number of people come together to engage in organized discourse.
The aim of a meeting could be:

- To provide information
- To form an opinion
- To make decisions

Those who take part in a meeting will each have a certain task to fulfil. A meeting will include:

- The chair: the chairman/chairperson (presides over the meeting)
- The secretary (writes the minutes)
- The other participants

Sometimes these tasks are taken in turns. Each participant gets to chair the meeting or be the secretary on some occasion. Before a meeting an agenda is drawn up. The outcomes of the meeting are laid down in the minutes.

The badly prepared meeting can be quite chaotic, particularly if the agenda has not been provided beforehand. It should be realized that a meeting can be quite a costly affair because it takes the participants away from their daily work. They may even have to travel some distance. A meeting of a couple of hours with a number of participants can easily cost a few thousand dollars, especially if traveling costs and time are taken into account. This is why meetings should be efficient and focused. This chapter can be a help and its various sections could be used as a checklist.

⬤7.2 Preparing for the meeting

Organize

The chair is responsible for the organization and management of the meeting. Good preparation is essential. Before holding the meeting the chair should *organize* a number of things, some of which are very practical:

- Determine the purpose of the meeting.
- If necessary, ask permission from management. In most organizations you need a mandate to call a meeting.
- Determine the time and place of the meeting, taking account of the participants' travelling times and ease of access to the meeting place. If necessary, provide an itinerary showing how to get to the meeting place.
- Book the room and any aids needed for the meeting, arrange refreshments, and if required, lunch.
- Draw up the **agenda** (see section 6.3).
- Decide *who will take the minutes* and inform that person well before the start of the meeting. The **secretary** should be somebody who knows the organization well, since this will mean he has some knowledge of the topics under discussion. Make sure there is a replacement secretary available. Secretaries often happen to have a pressing arrangement just before the meeting.
- Send notice of the meeting, the agenda and any **meeting-related documents** to the participants well before the meeting. If there are a lot of documents or they are sizeable, this could be (say) one week beforehand. Avoid as much as possible handing out documents during or just before a meeting. If this is unavoidable, a time out to allow reading the docu-

ments should be called. All participants should be given a fair chance to
read the documents.

7.3 The meeting's agenda

The chair or the secretary draws up the agenda in consultation with others.
This involves the following:
- Making an inventory of the topics for the meeting and consulting those
  who will most likely be present.
- Deciding on the topics to be put on the agenda.
- Determining the order in which the topics should be dealt with. You could
  decide to deal with the most important topics first or arrange the items
  in some other logical order. The most important items first is to be
  preferred if there are participants who have to leave early.
- If desired, setting a time limit for each point on the agenda.
- Drawing up the actual agenda (see Fig. 7.1).
- Not all of the points on this agenda need be necessary.
- Any other business. During this agenda item, the meeting's participants
  can put forward a topic for discussion. It is usual for the chair to ask at
  the beginning of the meeting whether anybody wants to make a contribution to that item of the agenda.

FIGURE 7.1 The agenda

Agenda for the meeting of the project group	Head section with the factuel details
Subject: .... Date: .... Time: .... Place: .... Those present: .... Chair .... Secretary	
1 Opening 2 Minutes of the previous meeting 3 Correspondence 4 Announcements	Introduction
5 Main topic 1 (......minutes) 6 Main topic 2 (......minutes) 7 Main topic 3 (......minutes) 8 Any other business	Main topics
9 Decisions 10 Questions without notice 11 Close	Conclusion
Appendices:	

The MS Word model "Agenda" can be downloaded from the website
accompanying this book.

If information will be provided during the meeting in the form of a *presenta-*   **Presentation**
tion, it is advisable to read Chapter 10: "Holding a presentation".

7.4 The meeting itself

During a project meeting, every participant plays a different role. Chapter 2 discussed the project roles of project manager, project member, user and sponsor as well as how to effectively brainstorm, negotiate and make decisions. In order to function well as a project group, it is essential that team agreements be made during the first project meeting and that members be aware of their own Belbin roles. It is therefore advisable to reread Chapter 2 at this point.

Belbin roles

Chair

The *chair* (chairman/chairperson) presides over the project meeting. His tasks are the following:
- Opening the meeting formally
- Checking the roll
- Ensuring that people do not deviate from the subject and cutting short anyone who goes off on their own topic
- Introducing each point on the agenda
- Leading the discussions
- Making sure all of the participants have a say
- Keeping an eye on the time
- Giving a short summary of all points on the agenda, including
  - **Decisions** *made*
  - **Action points**
  (This could be done by the secretary instead)
- Noting the topics that are to be put on the agenda again at the next meeting
- Calling for a short break if the participants request it
- During "Other business", asking every participant whether he has a question or a short announcement
- Formally closing the meeting. A meeting should not be left to peter out

The chair can exert quite a bit of influence on the business of a meeting. If he is primarily concerned with managing the meeting and less with the contents of the meeting, he is termed a *technical chair*.

Technical chair

Secretary

The *secretary* or minute secretary is preferably seated next to the chair and makes notes of the discussions. If there are any loose ends at the conclusion of an agenda item, the secretary may ask for clarification. It could be useful to have the secretary give a short summary at the conclusion of each agenda item.

7.5 After the meeting

It is advisable for the secretary to write up the minutes as soon as possible after the meeting, when things are still fresh in the memory. There might be *action points* that have to be acted on quickly. The minutes may be concise or extensive (this should be discussed with the chair) and are set out in the same way as they were on the agenda.

Action points

The minutes of work meetings and project meetings should at least contain the following points: (see Fig. 7.2.)
- The head section with the factual details. These are essentially the same details as those in the agenda but with a few additions:

- The names of those present
- The names of those who were absent. Indicate whether they were absent with or without notification (optional).
- The date the minutes were made
- The announcements
- A short summary of each point on the agenda
- A list of decisions
- A list with action points including:
  - The action to be taken
  - The deadline
  - The person responsible for carrying it out

A list such as this is a great help for the minutes of project meetings. The project manager can use it to better manage the project members and to take action if the tasks have not been carried out, leaving no room for excuses like "I didn't know I was supposed to do that" or "Did it have to be finished already?" Action points stay on the list until dealt with.

FIGUUR 7.2 The minutes

Minutes of the meeting of the project group	Head section
Subject:	
Date: .... Time:	
Place:	
Those present: .... Chair	
.... Secretary	
....	
Absent: .... with notification	
.... without notification	
Minutes ready:	
1 Opening	Introduction
2 Minutes of the previous meeting	
3 Correspondence	
4 Announcements	
Per main topic, possibly a short report on the discussion	Main topics
Decisions:	Results
....	
Action points: .... to be done by .... outcome	
.... to be done by .... outcome	
Appendices:	

Work or project meetings do not usually have to contain a verbatim report of what was said by the participants. Before the minutes are sent off they should be checked by the chair. After any corrections have been incorporated, they should be sent off as soon as possible to all the participants and other interested parties. During the next meeting comments on the minutes will be called for.

The MS Word model "Minutes" can be downloaded from the website accompanying this book.

Assignments

7.1   A meeting has been arranged with five project members who are specialists in their field and who live in various places in the Netherlands. The meeting will take three hours and will be held in Utrecht. Two of the five participants live in Groningen (a distance of 200 km), one lives in The Hague (80 km) and another in Eindhoven (100 km). The project manager is the chairman and he lives in Utrecht. A room has been booked somewhere in Utrecht. The project manager has already spent an entire day preparing for the meeting. Writing and reading the minutes takes up a total of four hours.
a First, make a global estimate of the total costs of this meeting.
b Next, calculate the exact costs. The hourly rate is 75 euros. Any other costs should be estimated.

7.2   Draw up an agenda following the model provided in this chapter for:
a A meeting between the project manager and the project team
b A meeting of the steering committee
c A meeting between the project manager and the sponsor
d A meeting you yourself have to attend in the near future

7.3   Using the model provided in this chapter, write the minutes of the most recent meeting you have attended.

7.4   List a number of characteristics a good chairperson should possess.

7.5   Decisions often have to be made during project meetings. A number of ways of reaching agreement are listed below. List the advantages and disadvantages of each of them.
a The decision is made by one person (the project manager or an expert, for instance).
b A majority decision is made based on votes cast.
c The decision must be unanimous: everybody has to be in agreement.
d A compromise decision. This is a decision that is obtained by taking all the options and combining them into a collective solution.

7.6   Form groups to discuss the following statements:
a It is preferable to have the project manager chair the project team meeting.
b If there are no topics for the agenda it is not necessary to hold the weekly project team meeting.
c Time spent in preparation for a meeting is more than regained during the meeting itself.
d During a meeting on problems associated with a project it is important to find out who caused those problems.

8
Conducting interviews

The project members are often likely to need information from others while they are carrying out research during the course of the project. In such circumstances, the project worker will make use of interviewing techniques. An interview is a conversation usually between two people in which the interviewer obtains information from the interviewee. The interviewee is likely to be an expert in the field and have some information that the interviewer requires.

This chapter provides a number of practical tips for preparing for an interview, conducting it and writing up a report afterwards.

8.1 Types of interviews

Interviews range in type from having a predetermined format to the open interview.

Questionnaire

With the first type, the interviewer will have formulated the questions beforehand and set them in a certain order (as a *questionnaire*, for example).

There are certain advantages to a predetermined interview:
- The interviewer can prepare thoroughly for the interview.
- The answers can be processed systematically.
- The interviewer is in control of the discussion.

The disadvantage is that the conversation will proceed according to a rigid pattern with the possible consequence that some important information may not be obtained.

Open interview

During an *open interview* the interviewer will not stick to a set questionnaire or a certain question sequence. He will, however, have formulated and listed some points of attention. There is likely to be much less formal preparation.

The advantages are as follows:
- The information collected will not be as restricted.
- The interviewee usually regards this type of interview as pleasant.

The disadvantages are:
- It may take an inexperienced interviewer a lot of time to collect the important information. A second session may even be required.
- There is a greater chance of misunderstandings occurring.
- The answers are more difficult to process systematically.

An in-between type of interview has proven its worth, and suggestions on how to go about such an interview are given in the sections below.

8.2 The three stages of an interview

An interview consists of three aspects:
1 Preparation
2 Execution
3 Reporting

These three aspects are explained in chronological order below.

Preparing for the interview

You can hold an interview alone or in pairs, in which case one person asks the questions and the other takes notes. Working in pairs is recommended for those who have not had much experience with interviewing. A division of tasks makes it easier for the interviewer to concentrate on the conversation. The interview can also be recorded on tape. If you use tape, you should remember that the interviewee might be less prepared to talk

openly about certain matters because "everything he says may be used against him". The following activities should be carried out before holding an interview:
- The objectives of the interview should be formulated.
- A suitable candidate should be found.
- Information about the interviewee such as name, company, position and work situation should be gathered.
- The interviewer should try to place himself mentally in the situation of the interviewee.
- If necessary, the interviewer should arrange to be introduced to the person being interviewed by somebody who knows him or her well.
- After making an appointment with the interviewee:
  - Explain why you want this interview.
  - Determine a place and time.
  - Book a suitable venue if necessary.
  - Arrange refreshments.
  - Agree on a starting and a finishing time.
  - If there will be two people conducting the interview, the interviewee needs to know this.
  - If you want to use recording equipment you should ask the interviewee's permission first. It is advisable to take notes during an interview even when recording equipment is used. These notes can be a help in asking relevant questions during the interview and they make writing a report afterwards easier and less time consuming.
  - You could even at this stage make an appointment for a further interview.
- If necessary, confirm the appointments in writing.
- Read up on the subject of the interview by consulting the professional literature, reports and earlier interviews, if available.
- Draw up a list of topics.
- Note down a few questions for each topic. These may be either open questions or multiple choice questions.
- These questions could also be sent to the interviewee beforehand.

Conducting the interview
Structure the interview as follows:
- Introduction
- The interview itself
- Conclusion

The topics for discussion during the *introduction* could include: **Introduction**
- Something about yourself
- The position and the activities of the person interviewed. This is a good ice breaker. Try to establish some rapport with the interviewee. Be neutral and open.
- The time limit. Set one at this stage.
- The purpose of the interview
- The topics that will be treated during the interview. Run quickly through them.

During the interview itself, you will be *looking for answers* to your questions. **During the** The following suggestions may be useful: **interview**
- Do not talk down or up to the person being interviewed.

- Keep your questions brief, clear and concise.
- You could explain why you are asking a particular question.
- Be critical and not too easily satisfied with an answer.
- Listen carefully to the answers.
- Make clear that you understand what is being said ("So what you are saying is that….").
- If necessary, ask follow-up questions.
- Write down the answers.
- Stay in charge of the interview: many people enjoy being interviewed and can tell interesting anecdotes and stories.
- It is important that you – and certainly the interviewee – do not stray from the topic.
- Try to get as many exact figures as you can. You could, for instance, ask how long a certain situation has been in place. People being interviewed sometimes exaggerate the importance of current problems. You then run the risk of being informed primarily about "the problem of the day".

Conclusion

At the *conclusion* of the interview, round things off:
- Give a summary of the interview. This will reduce the risk of misunderstandings. If there are two people conducting the interview, this summary is best done by the person who has made the notes.
- If relevant, schedule the next interview.
- Confirm any other arrangements that have been made.
- Say that you will send a report of the interview to the person you have talked to and ask him whether he is prepared to give his comments on it. Make an arrangement about the way the report is to be written (see the next section).

Writing a report of the interview

Interview report

After the interview, the notes have to be made into an *interview report*. This should contain the following items:
- Head section containing date, place, name of the interviewer, name of the interviewee, subject of the interview.
- The factual information in a structured form.

There are a number of ways to make a report of an interview:
- It could be a verbatim report of the interview, in chronological order as much as possible.
- The interview could be represented in point form that includes only the highlights.
- The information obtained during the interview could also be presented in a structured and cohesive report.

If the interview report is required for a project, it is best to use the third manner of reporting.

Assumptions

Should anything remain unclear, you could try and call the interviewee to obtain additional information. If you have had to make some *assumptions*, you should mark these clearly as such in the text. This will alert the interviewee and prompt a response, which will then give you the required clarity.

Send a copy of the report to the interviewee and ask him to reply within a reasonable time. Incorporate any comments in the final report and, if appropriate, also send a final copy to the interviewee.

Assignments

8.1 Prepare for an interview, conduct it and report on it in the way that is suggested in this chapter. The report should be structured and cohesive. The interview should preferably be carried out by two people. Find somebody who is prepared to be interviewed by you. The report should be handed in to your trainer/teacher. You could consult your trainer or teacher about your choice of subject. Some suggested candidates and topics for an interview are as follows:

a A project manager about the way his/her project is managed (read Chapter 5 before conducting the interview)

b A researcher about the subject of his or her research

c A technician about his or her duties

d An artist about his or her work

e A doctor about how he or she organizes the practice and invoicing

f A nurse about his or her daily activities

g A computer programmer about his or her latest project

h A systems manager about his or her network

i A director or a manager about his or her firm

j A personnel manager about the tasks of his or her department

k A salesman about his or her department

l An administrator or an accountant about he or she work

m A quality manager about the handbook his or her has written

n A fellow student about his or her practical training or final project

o Your own choice

8.2 For this assignment, you and a small group interview an expert from a different field. You can choose from the topics given in the previous assignment or consult with your trainer/instructor about choosing a different topic. The results of the interview are then drawn up in an interview report (as an article, for example) and presented by the entire group. The interview should be conducted by two or three persons, each of whom assumes one of the following roles:
- The interviewer leads the interview.
- The minute secretary takes notes.
- The observer is responsible for the presentation.
- The roles of "minute secretary" and "observer" are both taken on by one person if the group has only two people in it.

Naturally the minute secretary and observer are also allowed to ask questions.

The interview
- First reread the recommendations from Chapter 7.
- To prepare for the interview, draw up a list of questions.

- Interview the expert.
- Draw up an interview report or write an article.

The presentation for other groups
- Use the recommendations from Chapter 10.
- Prepare the presentation using sheets or a beamer.
- Hold the presentation.

Additional presentation requirements
- The presentation should have a maximum of X sheets and last no longer than Y minutes. Discuss this with your trainer.
- Present the results of the interview in logical order. Do not simply "read" the answers to the questions asked!
- In conclusion, talk about the interview itself.

a How did the interview "go"?
b What kinds of things did you notice?
c Did you enjoy it?
d Did you understand everything? If not, what did you not understand?
e What did you find difficult? Easy?

9
Writing a report

After a project or piece of research has been completed, the results have to be conveyed to others. This may be done in writing or in the form of an oral presentation. The advantage of a written report over an oral presentation is that the subject can be treated in much greater detail and those interested in the subject have a tangible source to refer back to.
Writing a report is time-consuming. Reading a report can also be time-consuming. If a report is difficult to read, the reader will be tempted to put it away without finishing it. The writer's work will then have been in vain.
A report should therefore be clear and easy to read.

This chapter gives suggestions and instructions on how to write a good report. Matters of formulation and style fall outside the scope of this book.

9.1 Preparing to write the report

Before you start writing, make sure you are thoroughly prepared. This section lists the things to bear in mind.

- Determine what the report will be about. Try to formulate the **subject** as precisely as possible.
- Determine the report's **objectives**. They could be to provide information to other colleagues, interested parties or prospective team members, or to convince them of something. A report can also serve the purpose of giving an account of the results of the project to the sponsor.
- Determine who the **readers** are likely to be. When you are writing the report it is a good idea to keep the composition of the reading public and how informed they are in mind.
- Find out what sort of **structure** the report should have. A structure you could use for the project report is illustrated in this chapter.
- Find out what **layout conventions** your organization uses. These could be:
  - A stipulated layout for headers and footers, stipulated fonts and line spacing. Never put your own name in a header or footer.
  - Stationary with the organization's logo.
- Determine the maximum number of pages (in consultation with the sponsor).
- *Your tools*: after you have an idea of what company expects, find out whether **the right appliances** are actually available:
  - What word processor is recommended and/or available?
  - What printer (laser printer, color printer) is recommended and/or available? While you are drafting the report, select the printer that the report will be printed on as the standard printer.
  - What illustrations are available? Do they have to be made? Is the software required to do so available within the company?

9.2 Putting the report together

Time schedule

Find out when the report has to be ready by and then draw up a time schedule for writing it. If you are writing a report as part of a project, you could base the schedule on the project plan.

Writing a report involves four steps:

1. Collecting the data
2. Organizing the data
3. Writing the report
4. Checking the report

These steps are described in the following sections.

Collecting the data

Some important sources of data include:

- Earlier reports, accounts and memos
- Books and articles
- The Internet
- Your own research
- Information derived from interviews with people who are experts in the field (See Chapter 7, "Conducting interviews")

Organizing the data

Collect as much of the main information as you can and organize it. Draw up the *first outline* on the basis of this. This should contain a list of the topics the report will deal with.

First outline

The information should be arranged in a logical train of thought and structured in an orderly fashion. Keep the structure as set out in Section 9.3 in mind while you are doing this.

After you have decided on the general approach, draw up the *second outline*. This should set out a:

Second outline

- Chapter-by-chapter (or section-by-section) breakdown
- Breakdown within each chapter (into subsections or main headings)
- Breakdown into paragraphs (roughly what each paragraph will deal with without going into any detail at this stage).

It is a good idea to ask the sponsor to approve the second outline. One of the pitfalls of drafting is going into too much detail before the overall outline has become clear.

Writing the report

Points to consider when writing:

- Make sure the report stands on its own. The reader should not have to consult other literature to understand it.
- Divide it into chapters/sections and main headings/subsections, each built up of a varying number of paragraphs. Avoid making these too long. Make sure that each paragraph deals with one topic only and organize them in logical order.
- Avoid long and complicated sentences. Aim for a maximum length of between fifteen and twenty words. You will probably find that a long sentence can be divided into two shorter sentences.
- Write in a style your readers will understand.
- Be consistent in your style of writing. For example, avoiding addressing your audience in the "I" form, then the "we" form, then in an impersonal form. A text for professional purposes is usually best written in an impersonal style.
- If you introduce a new concept, you should explain it to your readers before going on to use it. This could be done in a footnote.
- Avoid double negatives (such as "It is not impossible for...").
- Do not bother too much about the layout while you are writing. This is best left to the end or to an expert.
- Make sure your grammar is correct and you have spelled everything correctly. Otherwise, your readers might be distracted from the content. Use the spelling check and the thesaurus in your word processor.
- Use a layout that facilitates reading, do not make the blocks of text too large and make sure the line distance is not too small.

Checking the report

Check to see whether you are still on track by asking yourself the following questions:

- Does the report give an answer to the problem?
- Are the pages numbered? Do they agree with the table of contents?
- Is the structure logical and well-balanced? Are things presented in the right order?

It is a good idea to ask others to read the report when it is done and provide critical feedback.

9.3 The structure of the report

How a report is structured depends on the report's objectives. The following structure is a useful one. (See Fig. 9.1)

FIGURE 9.1 The report

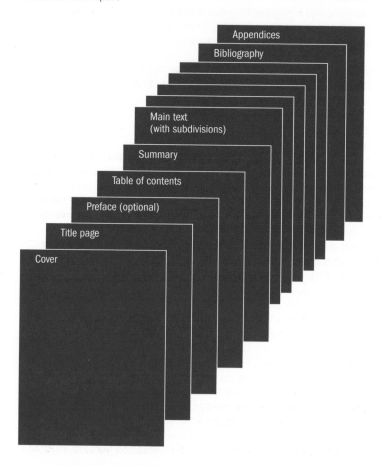

The cover
The first thing the reader sees is the cover of the report. It should be made of heavier paper than the rest of the report.
The cover should show the following:
- A short title
- A subtitle (optional)
- The name of the sponsor or organization
- Place and date
- The name of the author or authors and their job titles (optional)

Depending on whether it concerns an internal, external or personal publication, the cover could also show:
- The company or organization that commissioned the project
- The institution where the research was carried out

The title page
All the details on the cover are repeated on the title page. It may also include such things as a copyright statement or in the case of a confidential or classified report, a remark about limited distribution.

The preface (optional)
The preface mentions matters that are not part of the actual contents of the report such as:
- The report's history/background
- Something about the author
- Acknowledgements
- An indication of the public the report is directed at

If desired the preface can be written in the first person and signed.

The table of contents
The contents should be listed on a separate page and include the preface, the summary and the chapters/sections (broken down into main headings/subsections) accompanied by the relevant page numbers.
Only the starting page number of each chapter is given. If you have divided the report into chapters, sections, subsections and sub-subsections, only list three of these levels in the table of contents (Section 3.1 may be included, 4.2.4 could possibly be, but not 5.2.3.1).
If a word processor is used, the table of contents (including the page numbers) can be *generated automatically*. **Automatically generated**

The summary
Not every reader will have the time to read the report in full. The summary should be comprehensible even for those who have not read the report itself. The main points should be included in the summary:
- The reason for the report
- The problem
- Proposed solutions
- Why these solutions have been proposed
- The main conclusions and recommendations

Even if the report itself is not written in English, it is advisable to include an *English* summary. **English**

9.4 The main contents and finishing touches to the report

If it is a sizeable text, it should be divided up into *sections* and subsections/main headings (each of which consisting of a varying number of paragraphs): the structure of the report. A very large report could be divided up into chapters, sections and so on. Each section should be **Sections** comparable in level and subsections/main headings should be logical subdivisions of the chapters/sections. In addition to the main text, we will also be discussing how to put the finishing touches on a report.

Main text
How the chapters/sections are arranged will depend on the nature of the report. In the main text the chapters could be arranged as follows:

1 Introduction
A report should stand on its own, without appendices or other reports. If appropriate, other reports could be summarized briefly.

Context
It should contain a short description of the *context* or background against which the report was written. While the author might think that these things are self-evident, they may not be to the reader. He should be able to deduce what it is all about from the introduction.

Objectives
Make the *objectives* of the report clear. Why was it written? The answer could be to provide recommendations, documentation or an evaluation.

Problem
If the report's purpose is to suggest solutions to a problem, that *problem* should be formulated concisely. This can be difficult to do and should be done in consultation with the sponsor or supervisor.

Structure
It may be advisable to give some information relating to the *structure* of the report so that the reader knows what he or she can expect.
The subject should be outlined. What is included in the report and what is not should be stated.

2 Definition of the problem
The problem should be described and defined in detail, if necessary by dividing it into a number of "sub-problems".

3 Short description of the working method used
What was the author's approach? How was the data collected? Who else collaborated on the report?

4 Research
This part describes the research itself, the interim results and so on. The description of the research should be structured coherently and be complete. This part could consist of several chapters/sections.

5 Results and conclusions
The results and conclusions should follow logically from the previous chapters/sections.

6 Recommendations
Some recommendations on the basis of the results and conclusions might be made. The author can use this section as a forum for his or her personal opinion on the subject.

Bibliography
Any report will include references to publications by other people. These may include previously published reports, books or articles.

Various
conventions
The list of consulted publications should be arranged either alphabetically or in the order in which they are referred to in the text. There are *various conventions* you could follow. Whichever one you choose, be consistent in

the way you use it. This also applies to the title references. One convention governing title references is as follows:

- For a book: author or authors, title, edition, publisher, year of publication, page numbers or chapter
- For an article from a periodical: author or authors, date of publication, title of the article, name of the journal, volume (underlined or in italics), page numbers.

Appendices

Documents that would make a text difficult to read if they were included – such as complicated drawings, examples, detailed descriptions – should be added as an appendix.

Appendices should be numbered consecutively and have a heading. These appendices can be referred to in the main text and should also be included in the table of contents.

Finishing touches

The spelling should be checked and the report read with a critical eye by a third party. Make sure the layout is good, have the report bound and have it distributed.

9

Assignments

9.1 If your project consists of a piece of research or a survey, the findings could be published in the form of a report. Give a number of reasons why you would want to give an oral presentation on the outcomes of your project in addition to a written report of the desired quality.

9.2
  a What is the difference between the objectives of a research report and the definition of the problem?
  b Give an example of an objective and the associated problem definition.

9.3 A report can be used as a basis for an executive summary.
  a Explain why.
  b What topics are likely to be dealt with in an executive summary?

9.4 List a number of the characteristics of a good report.

9.5 Try to get hold of an actual report (either from one of your fellow students or colleagues, from the library or from the company's multimedia centre). Give an evaluation of that report based on the criteria described in of this chapter. Suggest improvements.

project

10
Holding a presentation

Throughout the entire course of the project as well as after it has been completed, people will need to be kept informed about what is going on. This can be done in writing or in the form of an oral presentation.

A presentation is a structured oral report on a clearly defined subject held by one or more people. A good presentation is an effective way of providing information and getting the audience on your side. Since you can highlight certain issues during the presentation, you can often present your case more convincingly than you would in writing.

The instructions and points to remember given in this chapter will assist you in preparing and holding an effective presentation.

⑩.① Organization and contents of a presentation

This section discusses the organization of the presentation, followed by the contents.

Organization of the presentation

When organizing a presentation, keep the following in mind:

- Determine the **time** and place of the presentation. Bear in mind the travelling times of the participants and the accessibility of the place. It is also a good idea to keep in mind that most people concentrate better in the morning than in the afternoon. A lot of energy goes into digesting a big lunch, so this is usually not a good time for holding a presentation.
- Estimate the time you will need. If your presentation is part of a meeting, you should determine how much time is at your disposal. You should not make your presentation too long; most people start to lose concentration after about half an hour.
- Book a suitable **room**. If you have a choice, get a room that does not have direct sunlight and that has a comfortable temperature. Bright sunlight will interfere with the visibility of your transparencies and a tropical temperature will distract your audience. Find out whether the room can be darkened.
- Find out what kind of **equipment** is available for the presentation. You might need a lectern, an overhead projector, a flip-over pad, a whiteboard or a computer-operated projector (beamer). If you plan to use equipment belonging to other people, you should book them well in advance.
- If necessary, make **arrangements** for refreshments or lunch.
- Find out about your audience. The contents of a presentation should be geared to that audience and their knowledge of the topic. A presentation at the end of a project will probably be held before an audience consisting of the members of the project team, the sponsor, the organization management team and others.
- A public presentation should be announced well in advance by means of notice boards and other media. If invitations will be sent to participants, they should be sent well in advance.

Contents of the presentation

Keep the following points in mind:

- Determine the **objectives** of your presentation. You might want to provide the audience members with information, get them on your side, motivate them, train them or sell them something. It could be a combination of these. If you want to get the audience on your side, it may be a good idea to go lobbying beforehand to make sure that you have some supporters in the audience.
- Determine the **topic** of discussion and how much time is available. Try not to overwhelm the audience with information. If time is short, you might not get as far as the crucial aspects of your conclusions and recommendations.
- Collect the **information** necessary for the presentation.
- If you have held presentations before, ask yourself whether they were successful. If you have made mistakes, use this knowledge to improve your next presentation.
- Make sure that your language style matches your audience. Everyone present should be able to follow the presentation. Avoid jargon as much as possible.

10

- Make up your mind as to whether you are going to read out or improvise using a list of main points. Unless you can read out the presentation extremely well, the audience will soon lose interest – and this should be avoided at all costs. If you are worried about losing track, you could write the key words of your main points on index cards.

🔟❷ Using an overhead projector or a beamer

The now somewhat outdated *overhead projector* uses transparencies or slides. The text and the illustrations are printed, drawn or written on them in black or colour. They are projected using a mirror onto a screen behind the speaker, so the speaker can remain facing the audience.

Overhead projector

A computer with presentation software and a projector – a *beamer* – is another option. The recommendations below apply to both options. In professional presentations, the layout of the transparencies or slides is usually the same, and may include the company logo, a heading at the top of each transparency, page numbers and the name of the speaker.

Beamer

EXAMPLE 10.1

Poor preparation

The following is a true story. A speaker steps onto the podium in front of an audience of about forty people. He has a whole stack of transparencies under his arm, and he starts by rummaging through them and muttering under his breath. He puts one of them on to the projector and says, "But, wait, you know all that..." and removes it immediately. He puts on the next transparency, mutters, "Hmm...this isn't all that important" and removes that one too. The third time he is lucky. This transparency – one showing a highly detailed table – is allowed to stay. However, since the letters are so small the words are unreadable.

So, when using transparencies or slides, keep the following in mind:
- Prepare your presentation well, do not show transparencies or slides that have nothing to do with the subject matter and make sure your transparencies are legible.
- The font should be large enough so that even the people in the back can read the transparencies. If you are using a computer, you will need a font size of at least 18 points for the text to be readable.
- Be careful what colours you use. Make sure there is enough contrast between the text and background.
- Make sure your **layout** is pleasing to the eye. Not every good presenter is a good graphic designer. It may be advisable to get someone to comment on the transparencies first. If the presentation is a very important one, you might get a professional designer to do them. Many companies like the house style to be followed. A template of the house style may be available for use on presentation software.
- Do not use too many transparencies or slides and do not change them too quickly. Give your audience the opportunity to read them properly.

10

- Do not put too much information on one transparency or slide. Out of a misplaced sense of economy, some people tend to put as much information on a transparency or slide as possible.
- One **grammatical mistake** is distracting but more than one is deadly. Your audience will instinctively start a "find the mistake" game and you will have lost their attention completely.
- When using computer **presentation software** such as PowerPoint, together with a special projector (beamer), you can create an impressive presentation with colourful sheets. There are all kinds of effects – even animation-that can be used. One click of the mouse and attractive images with special effects can be shown to a spellbound audience. You can also user a laser pointer to point on the screen. Since this equipment is connected to the USB port on a computer, making it possible to leaf through the slides of your presentation. Do not overdo it, however, because the content of the presentation is, after all, the main thing.
- If you are using a computer with a beamer for your presentation, consider having **back-up transparencies** for an overhead projector on hand. A lovely computer presentation going wrong because the projector bulb is broken or due to technical problems is not unheard of.
- Test beforehand in a room with an overhead projector whether your transparencies or slides are easy to read. Poor readability is distracting and annoying to the audience.
- If you are using software such as PowerPoint, it is possible to print the slides on paper in a reduced format (such as three slides above one another per page). There will then be room for notes next to each slide. These prints could be distributed as **handouts** to your audience before the start of your presentation to enable them to take notes. The disadvantage of this is that some of them are likely to start leafing through the slides and reading ahead, thereby becoming distracted. If your audience asks for a handout and you do not have any, you can always promise to have them sent by mail or to send the whole of the PowerPoint presentation as an e-mail attachment.

10.3 The structure of a presentation

You should structure your presentation along the following lines:
- Introduction
- Main body
- Conclusion

Keep a close eye on the length of your presentation. Inexperienced speakers have the tendency to include too much and, as a result, run out of time. You should already have taken the length into account during your preparation. You may want to have a dry run either in your study, in front of the bathroom mirror or in front of your family members. Time yourself, but remember that the actual presentation usually takes more time than the general rehearsal.

The introduction
What should you deal with in your introduction?
- Attract your audience's attention by telling a little anecdote or a joke or making an informal remark. In American literature this is referred to as "**Hey you!**".

- Introduce yourself, state the purpose of the presentation and briefly outline the topic. This gives the audience the opportunity to mentally prepare for what is to come.
- State the **main points** of your presentation. List them on a separate transparency or slide.
- Indicate how you plan to deal with questions that might arise. If people interrupt by asking questions, you can lose track of your train of thought. Some people ask questions just to show off their knowledge of the subject, not because they want to actually get an answer. This can be very annoying. It is best to postpone any questions until after the presentation. This applies particularly if you have little experience in holding presentations.

Main body

How should you *structure* the main body of your presentation?   **Structure**
- Make sure the presentation is clearly structured. One possibility is:
  - Cause and effect
  - Chronological order of events
  - Question and answer
  - Proposition, discussion, conclusion
- If you are talking about a project, you will probably use the project plan as the starting point.
- Discuss your topic according to your chosen structure.
  - Give a brief summary after each subtopic.
  - With each new subtopic, indicate its place in the table of contents you provided at the beginning. You could use the introduction transparency to do this.

10

Conclusion

To round off the presentation:
- Give a summary of the main points.
- State your conclusions and repeat them.
- If you can, end on a **catchy note**, i.e. make the conclusion a memorable one. This can be a humorous remark or a one-liner that sums up the whole presentation. You could also refer back to the anecdote from the beginning of your talk. A good conclusion will be remembered by your audience and helps them wind down.
- Give the audience the opportunity to ask questions.

Clearly structure the transparencies or slides

Make sure your transparencies or slides are sorted into a suitable order. A useful order is as follows (see Figure 10.1):
- A **title slide or transparency** with perhaps the title of the presentation, the name of the organization and your own name. You can also use this transparency/slide (or the next one) to capture the attention of the audience. It could be a cartoon, film clip or illustration.
- A **table of contents**. This shows your audience how you are going to structure your presentation.
- The slides or transparencies showing the **points** as dealt with in the main body of the presentation. After you have shown these you could then "signpost" by showing the transparency or slide with the table of contents again. You can also include a visual element in a slide that indicates where exactly you are in the presentation.

- One or more slides with the summary, the conclusions and/or the recommendations in point form.

FIGURE 10.1 Structure of the presentation

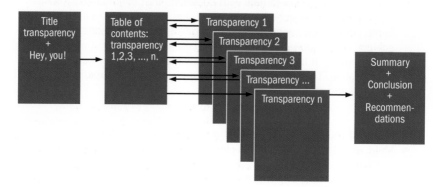

10.4 The presentation itself

Own behaviour When giving a presentation, you need to critically observe your *own behaviour*. Keep the following in mind:

- Whatever you do, be on time!
- Run through the points mentioned in Section 10.1 beforehand.
- Think positively: convince yourself that you have something important to say.
- Pay attention to how you say things (variation in pitch and tone, placing the right emphasis). If you tend to sound monotonous by nature, try and speak in an exaggerated manner (at least, what feels like exaggerated to you).
- Humour (of the appropriate type) can help you hold the attention of your audience.
- Do not speak too quickly. Pause between points and new topics.
- Stick to the structure of your presentation.
- Avoid using fillers or saying "uh".
- Use proper grammar.
- Speak clearly.
- Try to look confident, relaxed and sincere. If you find this difficult, it might help if you realize that your audience will be sympathetic if they are convinced that you have gone to considerable trouble to prepare the presentation.
- Look at your audience: this creates rapport. Avoid looking at the same person all the time or at the same corner of the room.
- If you are using an overhead projector and want to point to something, do it on the transparency and not on the projection screen. This keeps you facing your audience. You could also put an object on the transparency to indicate where you are. Do not use something that will roll off! There are laser pointers that enable you to point to things on the screen. Do not use these if you are very nervous, because any trembling of your hand will be magnified and the result will be a quivering circle of light on the screen. If you use a beamer you can use a laser pointer or mouse.

10

- Pay attention to your posture! Avoid putting your hands in your pockets or rubbing your nose all the time.
- Consciously use your **body language** to reinforce your message.
- Strike a happy balance between standing stiffly in one spot and pacing up and down all the time.
- Make sure the audience can see things like the overhead projector screen. Do not stand in front of it.
- Switch the beamer or the overhead projector off when you have finished using it. Most laser pointers have a button for "fading" the screen to black.
- If something goes wrong, you should not draw extra attention to it by apologizing or complaining about it.
- Give your audience the opportunity to ask questions, respond and discuss things. If you do not know the answer to a question, you could promise to provide the answer at a later date.
- Stick to your time limit. Your audience will probably not mind if you finish five minutes early, but they probably will if you take ten minutes longer. The chair may even cut the presentation short. If that happens, all your carefully prepared conclusions will have been in vain.

The website accompanying this book contains the "Presentation checklist" that covers the introduction, main body and conclusion as well the use of audiovisual aids, among other things.

Assignments

10.1 Keeping in mind the recommendations in this chapter, hold a presentation. Organize it as follows:
- Hold it in a group (there has to be an audience, after all). Each person in the group should take a turn delivering a presentation, the remainder forming the audience.
- Choose your topics. It is more fun if everybody has a different topic. Here are some suggestions:
  - A project you are (or have been) involved in
  - Scheduling theory
  - Using planning software
  - A book or article about project management you have read
  - A large project such as the Channel tunnel
  - Your company or your course of study
  - An interview you have done
  - A topic that your trainer assigns to you
  - A topic of your own choosing
  Discuss your choice of topic with your trainer/teacher.
- Decide on a time limit for a presentation (for example, no longer than 15 minutes).
- Decide how you plan to create the transparencies (by hand or on the computer). You might decide to use a beamer (or your trainer/teacher might decide you have to).
- Everybody then gives their presentation. You could hold presentations in sets of four.
- The audience evaluates the presentation while it is being given. The website accompanying this book contains a "Presentation checklist" that can be used.
- The members of the audience should give their feedback as soon as each presentation ends. Use the checklist.
- After all the presentations have been held, your trainer/teacher could assess them.

10.2 See assignment 8.2. This assignment involves not only conducting an interview but also holding a presentation.

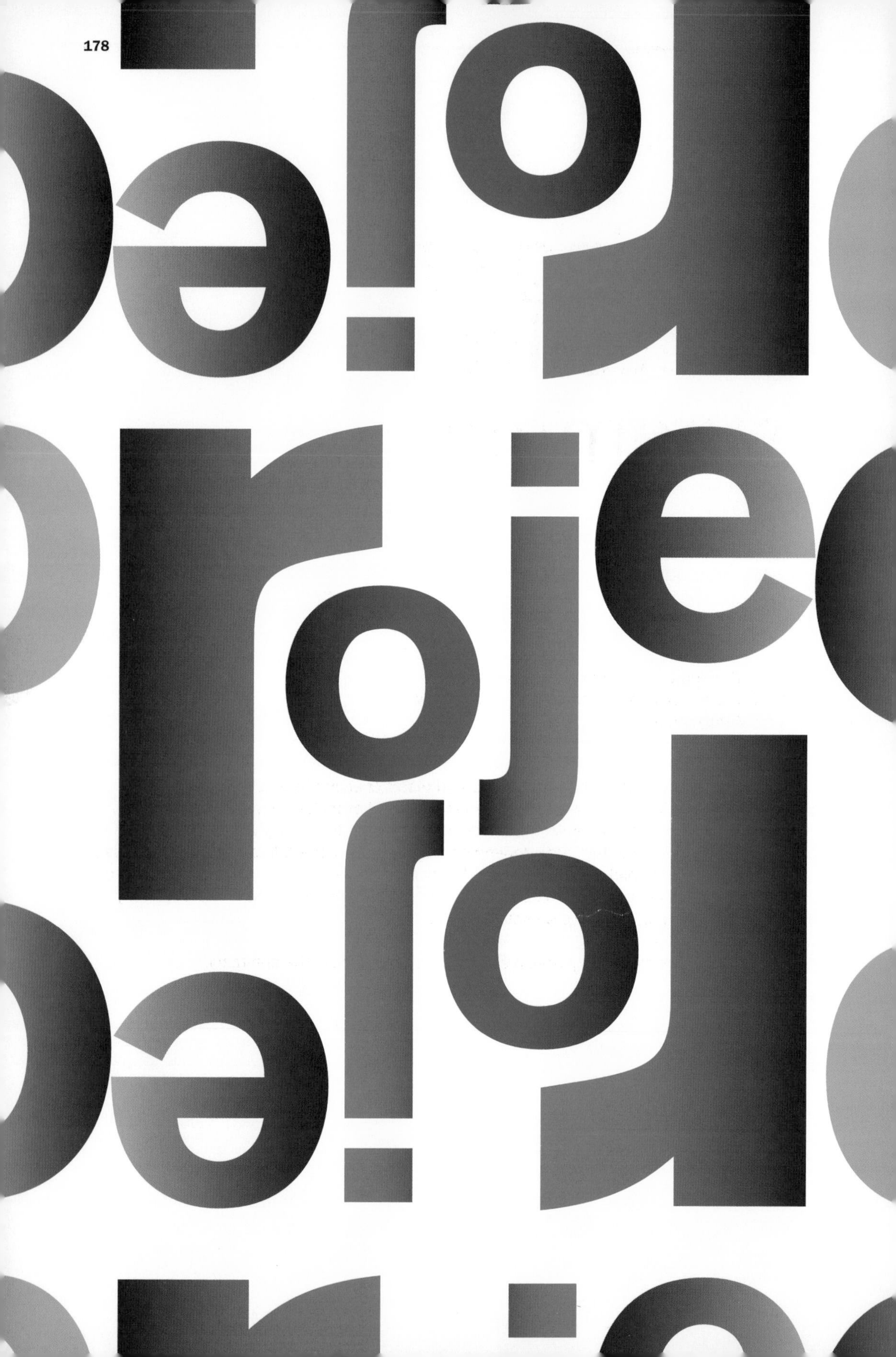

11
Making an executive summary

11

Large projects are often done in phases. At the end of each phase, the sponsor has to decide what to do next. Disappointing results or failed expectations may even mean the decision to terminate the project. Such decisions are made not only on the basis of the manager's experience; they also depend on information received. It is therefore essential, not only at the completion of the project, but also at the end of each phase of the project, that the sponsor have reliable information in an appropriate form. This information may take the form of an executive summary.

This chapter examines the purpose and structure of an executive summary.

⓫⓵ The purpose of an executive summary

Managers often do not have the time – or desire – to read lengthy reports. Both the interim and final results are therefore often summarized in the form of an executive summary by the project group. An executive summary should give a retrospective account of a finished part of the project, including an account of the results and conclusions. An executive summary should also be oriented towards the future, giving recommendations and *stating points* that require an executive decision. Fig. 11.1 shows this in diagram form.

FIGURE 11.1 The executive summary: looking back and looking ahead

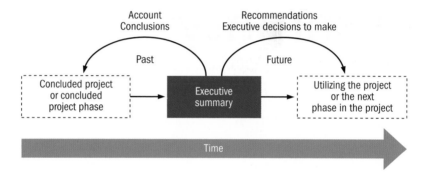

Executive summaries are particularly useful with large projects. Ask the sponsor whether one is required. Make sure you explain exactly what the purpose and the contents of an executive summary are.

Bear the reader in mind when you are writing an executive summary. It should not be too long, no more than 10 pages. It should be structured to be readable, and it should stand on its own; the reader should not have to refer to other literature.
After reading the summary, the manager should know how to proceed. This even applies to a manager who is relatively unfamiliar with the project.

⓫⓶ The components of an executive summary

This section deals with each of the main components of an executive summary. The structure of an executive summary is illustrated in Figure 11.2.

Title page
The title page of an executive summary should contain the following items:
• The term "Executive Summary"
• The name of the project
• A subtitle (optional)
• The name of the sponsor or organization
• Place name and the date
• The name of the author or authors
• The name of the author/s and, if desired, their job titles

FIGURE 11.2 The executive summary

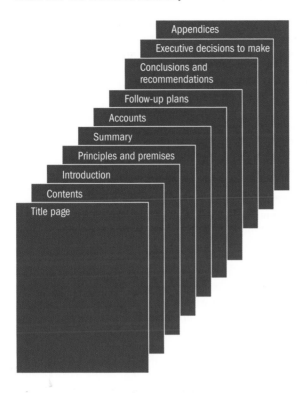

Contents
This should list all of the sections of the executive summary along with the page numbers. You could get your word processor to generate them.

Introduction
The introduction should briefly describe the purpose of the executive summary, refer to *contextual factors* and describe the following:

Contextual factors

- The project's objectives
- If the project is a research project, the research question
- The sponsor and assignee
- The project environment: something about the company or the department in which the project was carried out.
- The time span the report covers
- The project's commission or a reference to it (if relevant)

Principles, boundaries and working methods
The section on "Principles, boundaries and working methods" discusses the following:

- Principles and premises: what did the project involve; what did it not include?
- Changes to any earlier principles and premises
- A broad outline of the working method used

Summary of the results

This part should contain a summing up of and the rationale behind the results. The solutions the project has come up with up to this point should also be mentioned. This is not the same as the working method. If the project consists of a piece of research, the findings should be discussed here. The executive summary should contain enough information to allow management to make responsible and valid decisions.

Accounts

The "Accounts" section should describe the following:
- The products that the project team has delivered during the past period
- The costs of the project in terms of money and manpower
- A comparison of the actual state of affairs with the original plans: how much of the original plan has, in fact, been carried out, both in terms of duration and the use of resources such as labour and money.
- Any **discrepancies** between the original plan and the actual time and resources that have gone into it should be accounted for.

Follow-up plans

Cost/benefit

The "Follow-up plans" section should refer to the preliminary design of the next phase/follow-up project. The detailed design may be included in a supplement. There should also be a *cost/benefit* summary. A detailed cost/ benefit table may also be included as a supplement.

Conclusions and recommendations

Summary of
the results

The project group expresses its *own opinions* in the "Conclusions and recommendations" section. These should relate to the results given in the "Summary of the results" section (see above).
The following are included here:
- Conclusions
- Recommendations for the future
- Any problems likely to be encountered in the near future

Executive decisions to be made

Decisions

The project team will have worked intensively on the project up to this point. It will know all the ins and outs of the project. The organization's management team will have to make decisions based on the results they have been shown. It is one of the tasks of the project team to make it clear in the *executive summary* what decisions have to be made. The executive summary is a preliminary decision-making document. It is, in fact, a list of points on the basis of which the executive meeting determines what action has to be taken.

There will at least have to be executive decision making in relation to the following:
- An approval of the previous phase (in writing)
- A go-ahead for the next phase
- Continuation or disbanding of the project group

Other matters may also be involved. They may include:
- Purchase of new resources
- Recruiting staff
- Starting the next phase of the project

This section of the executive summary should be as detailed as possible.

Supplements/Appendices
The supplements or appendices could include more detailed information, including the following:
- The project plan for the next phases of the project
- A detailed cost/benefit overview

The executive summary should, however, stand on its own.

11

Assignments

11.1 Explain how an executive summary "says something" about the past.

11.2 Explain how an executive summary "says something" about the future.

11.3 In which part of an executive summary can you give your own opinion?

11.4 For each of the following hypothetical situations, make an executive summary according to the instructions given in this chapter.
   a Your practical training
   b Your thesis research
   c A project you had to carry out as part of your studies

Final Assignments

A number of additional cases can be downloaded from the website accompanying this book.

1   For each of the following hypothetical situations, make a project plan according to the instructions given in Chapter 5, "Drawing up a project plan". Try to really imagine the situation and make up any details you have to. This assignment is best carried out in groups of two or three people.

a You work in an office. Management has asked you to be the manager of a project aimed at computerizing the office. This involves buying computers and selecting and installing software (word processing, spreadsheet and e-mail). Write a project plan.

b The Economics Department of a university is located in an annex. The other departments (Engineering and Education) are located in the main building. The Executive Board has decided that the Economics Department should move to the main building one year from now. Write a project plan for the move.

c You run an environmental consultancy firm. A chemical company wants your firm to draw up an environmental research report on waste water purification. Write a project plan.

d You want to build a house. The first step is to design it in collaboration with an architect. The requirements have to be formulated and a suitable site selected and purchased. Plan the activities in phases. If possible, arrange an interview with someone who has gone through this process. Write a project plan.

e A metal construction firm is commissioned to build a metal frame bridge across the Rhine. The commission has to be approached as a project. Write a project plan.

f Your best friend is getting married and he wants to do it in style: coaches, wedding cake, dinner, reception, the works. Because you have had experience working on projects, he asks you to organize it all. You decide to tackle it as a project and write a project plan.

g You want to start a shop in computer accessories in your home town. You decide to tackle this in a structured fashion: as a project and with a project plan. The plan will include market research, setting up an administration system, consulting with suppliers, drawing up a business plan, registering with the Chamber of Commerce and recruiting employees. Keeping the various phases in mind, write a project plan.

h The Executive Board of a university wants to introduce a student information program for registering student grades. Students records are currently kept using a card file. The new system will be chosen from one of the currently available student information programs. Write a project plan.

i Two competing computer shops in your home town have decided to merge.

Both shops have not only a sales department but also a service department. The aim of the merger is to cut down on costs. Write a project plan.

j Come up with your own project and write a project plan.

2   Imagine that assignment 1 has also been carried out, either in part or
totally. Make an executive summary for the sponsor in accordance with the
instructions in Chapter 11.

3   Your group (between three and ten people) has been commissioned by your
supervisor or sponsor to carry out a project. Examples of similar projects
can be found in Chapter 1 and on the website.
The assignment is still somewhat vaguely defined. Your first tasks are to
specify exactly project result is required and put together a project group.
To do this well, refer back to Chapters 1 to 4 before starting the assignment. You'll need the other chapters of this book to ensure that your
project is a success.
Depending on the project, the assignment should take between 40 to 160
study hours. It should include all of the aspects listed below. If you wish to
change any of these aspects, you must first obtain permission from the
sponsor or your supervisor. You will have to divide up the tasks, bearing in
mind that not every team member will be involved in all of the activities.

a Set up the project organization (Chapter 2)
b Make a project plan.
   Note: make sure you do not leave out any of the sections of the project
   plan (see Chapter 5).
   If the sponsor or your supervisor considers a section of your project plan
   unnecessary, still include it, but add a comment saying that, in consultation
   with the sponsor, that particular section will not be dealt with in any further
   detail.
c The project plan should include schedules (see Chapter 4). If you draw
   them up by hand, make both a Gantt chart and a network diagram. Use
   planning software wherever you can.
d Write the project plan as if you were the project manager and are enthusiastic about the project.
e After you have drawn up a preliminary plan, discuss it with the sponsor
   and/or your supervisor. Afterwards, write the definitive project plan (see
   section 5.13.)
f The filing system should be organized as described in section 5.14.
g The time spent on the project by each team member should be recorded on
   a timesheet (see the sample "Time registration form" on the website
   accompanying this book). This timesheet should be handed in weekly to the
   project manager, who will use it to make a cumulative record for each team
   member to determine each member's contribution. The weekly review
   should be discussed with the sponsor and then filed (in the day-to-day files:
   see Chapter 5).
h Organize project meetings, including an agenda and minutes of the meeting
   (see Chapter 7.)
i Conduct interviews according to the procedure described in Chapter 8.
j Write a report (see Chapter 9.)
k Write an executive summary. This should be done after the project has
   been completed (see Chapter 11.)
l Hold a presentation on the results of the project (see Chapter 10.)

m Write one or more letters (see the website), perhaps to invite the sponsor to the presentation.

The final result of this assignment should be:
1 The definitive approved project plan
2 The final report on the findings. This report should be based on the system file.
3 An executive summary
4 An oral presentation on the project's outcome
5 The project's accounts as contained in the day-to-day files, including:
  – The provisional project plan
  – The project organization
  – Correspondence
  – The agendas and minutes of project meetings
  – The timesheets of all project workers
  – A cumulative weekly review per team member

6 The document files. This contains containing relevant information such as the following:
  – Intermediate results
  – Interview reports
  – Relevant information that has been gathered
  – Schedules and drawings
The supervisor will judge the project result based on these points.

4 You could approach any assignments you receive during your practical training as a project. Draw up a project plan in conjunction with the supervisor from the company where you are doing your practical training and your study supervisor. Try to apply as many of the tools and techniques from the second half of this book as you can (interviews, letters, presentations, etc.). Afterwards, write an executive summary.

5 Make an executive summary of your practical training.

6 Treat your final research project as a project. Make a project plan, applying as many of the techniques in the second half of this handbook as you can.

Appendix 1
Risk Analysis

- -

Section 3.12 focused on possible project risks. Step-by-step instructions were also given as to how to carry out a risk analysis for a project. The table below can also be used as a helpful resource. It is based on a method taken from *Handboek Informatieplanning* (Aarts, 1989). See the bibliography for details. The risks mentioned are of a general nature. Some of them may not apply to every field, and, since every field is potentially different as far as the risk factors are concerned, not every risk is included. You may need to add other, specific risks. The "weight" of the risks may also be considered. This will therefore have an effect on the overall score. The risk percentage calculated using the table is only a rough indication.

Risk	Value	Factor		Weight	Total risk
Time factor					
1 Estimated duration of the project	0–3 months	0			
	3–6 months	1	×	4	–
	more than 6 months	3			
2 Does the project have a definite deadline	no	0			
	flexible	2	×	4	–
	yes	4			
3 Is there sufficient time to complete the project within the set period?	more than enough	0			
	enough	1	×	4	–
	not enough	3			
Complexity of the project					
4 The number of functional subsectors involved	1	0			
	2	1	×	4	–
	3+	3			
5 The number of functional subsectors that will make use of the outcomes	1	0			
	2-3	1	×	2	–
	4	2			
6 Is it a new project or one that has been adapted?	minor adaptions	0			
	major adaptions	2	×	5	–
	new project	3			
7 To what extent do the present authorizations have to be adjusted?	not	0			
	minor extent	1			
	medium extent	2	×	5	–
	major extent	3			

- -

Risk	Value	Factor		Weight	Total risk
8 Are other projects dependent on this one?	no	0			
	yes, though the dead-lines are not tight	1	×	5	–
	yes, and the dead-lines are tight	3			
9 What sort of reception are the users likely to give it?	enthusiastic	0			
	noncommittal	1	×	5	–
	not interested	2			
10 Has the project been divided up into phases and is progress dependent on the coordination between them?	no	1			
	a little	2	×	3	–
	strongly	3			

The project group

11 Where do the project workers come from?	mainly internally	0			
	partly internally	1	×	4	–
	mainly externally	3			
12 Where is the project located?	1 location	0			
	1 to 3 locations	1	×	2	–
	more than 3 locations	2			
13 The number of projects taking up more than 80% of peak hours	1–5	0			
	5–10	2	×	5	–
	10+	4			
14 The balance between subject experts and project experts	good	0			
	average	2	×	5	–
	unfavourable	4			
15 Are the users involved in the project?	to a large extent	0			
	to a reasonable extent	1	×	3	–
	to a limited extent	3			

The project management

16 Does the project management team have any knowledge of the subject?	a lot	0			
	a reasonable amount	2	×	3	–
	little	4			
17 Does the project management have any knowledge of how to plan a project?	a lot	0			
	a reasonable amount	2	×	3	–
	little	4			
18 How much experience does the project manager have with projects like this?	a lot	0			
	a reasonable amount	1	×	3	–
	little	3			
19 Do the advisers have any knowledge of the field of research?	a lot	0			
	a reasonable amount	1	×	5	–
	little	3			
20 Do the subject experts have much knowledge of the field?	a lot	0			
	a reasonable amount	1	×	5	–
	little	3			

Risk	Value	Factor		Weight	Total risk
21 How involved in the project are the managers responsible for it?	very reasonably involved only slightly	0 2 5	× 	5	–
22 Is there any chance that the project team will change during the project?	little chance some chance big chance	0 2 5	× 	5	–
23 Is the project group using existing methods or creating its own methods?	only existing methods some existing methods no existing methods	0 2 4	× 	4	–
Project definition					
24 Are the project members sufficiently aware of the problems and objectives?	yes, everybody most of them not all of them	0 1 5	× 	5	–
25 Is the field of research sufficiently demarcated?	yes reasonably not clearly	0 2 5	× 	5	–
26 Is there sufficient demarcation between this project and other projects?	considerable reasonable insufficient	0 1 3	× 	4	–
27 Has enough time been reserved for coordination and decision-making?	considerable reasonable insufficient	0 1 3	× 	4	–
28 Are the boundaries clearly demarcated?	yes in general most of them are not no	0 1 3 5	× 	4	–
29 Are the boundaries limiting enough?	yes moderately no	0 2 5	× 	5	–

Risk percentage = $\dfrac{\text{total}}{\text{maximum score}} \times 100\%$ =

Rule of thumb: If the percentage is higher than 50% the project should not be carried out in this form.

 A spreadsheet model can be downloaded from the website, which can be used to carry out your risk analysis in MS Excel.

Appendix 2
Website

www.projectmanagement-english.noordhoff.nl

 This book is accompanied by a website, www.projectmanagement-english.noordhoff.nl, which contains two sections: one for students and one for instructors. As well as additional information on this book, various files can also be downloaded from the website (see below). If you are downloading a PDF file, you will need to have Adobe Acrobat Reader in order to read it. This program can be downloaded free of charge from www.adobe.com.

1 Extra theory
To keep the size of this book manageable, two of the less frequently used chapters from the previous edition have been moved to the website. Owners of this book may download the "Writing letters" and "Formulating a project quote" chapters from the website free of charge.

2 Mini-Course on MS Project
When planning a project, it is sometimes useful to use a planning program like MS Project. A complete mini-course on MS Project can be downloaded as a PDF file from the website accompanying this book. This way you can teach yourself the most important functions of MS Project. Obviously this means you must own or have access to this program. A number of sample schedules for use within MS Project are also available.

3 Checklists
Using a checklist in PDF format can help you check documents for completeness, thereby monitoring their quality. Checklists are available on the website for conducting an initial interview, holding a presentation, carrying out a stakeholder analysis and monitoring the completeness of a project plan.

4 Calculations models in MS Excel
MS Excel can be used to carry out calculations. Calculation models are available for keeping track of time spent (two documents), formulating a risk analysis and making a simple schedule.

5 Document models in MS Word
A number of MS Word models are included on the website to simplify your work and ensure a good layout. Documents are available for drawing up an agenda, taking minutes, writing a project proposal, making a project plan, writing a project progress report and writing a weekly report.

6 PowerPoint presentation accompanying the book
The website contains a PowerPoint presentation with a planning animation. There is also a PowerPoint presentation available for instructors, which can be adapted as necessary – provided the source is credited – for use in the classroom.

7   Cases

The cases can be used as a basis for practicing writing a project plan.

8   Instructor materials

In addition to the PowerPoint presentation, these materials include the answers to the assignments, a sample syllabus, cases and a correction model for a project plan. The website also provides access to an exam database.

Bibliography

Aarts, A.F.H. (1989). *Handboek Informatieplanning*. The Hague: Directie Economisch Beheer Koninklijke Landmacht.

Andersen, E.S. (1989). *Doeltreffend projectmanagement*. Utrecht: A.W. Bruna.

Anthonisse, P.M. (1993). *Project Management Methodology*. Rijswijk: Lansa Publishing.

Belbin, R.M. (1999). *Managementteams. Over succes- en faalfactoren voor teams*. Schoonhoven: Academic Service.

Belbin, R.M. (1999). *Teamrollen op het werk*. Schoonhoven: Academic Service.

Best, K. de (1990). *Communicatietechnieken*. Groningen: Wolters-Noordhoff.

Blom, S. & Storm, P. (1993). *Effectief projectmanagement*. Groningen: Wolters-Noordhoff.

Comfort, J. e.a. (1990). *Professioneel rapporteren*. Groningen: Wolters-Noordhoff.

Covey, S.R. (1995). *De zeven eigenschappen van effectief leiderschap*. Amsterdam: Contact.

Gerritsma, M. & Grit, R. (2009). *Zo doe je een risicoanalyse*. Groningen: Noordhoff Uitgevers.

Gerritsma, M. & Grit, R. (2009). *Zo maak je een kwaliteitsplan*. Groningen: Noordhoff Uitgevers.

Gerritsma, M. & Grit, R. (2010). *Zo maak je een personeelsplan*. Groningen: Noordhoff Uitgevers.

Gevers, T. (1998). *Praktisch projectmanagement*. Schoonhoven: Academic Service.

Goldratt, E. (1999). *De zwakste schakel*. Utrecht: Het Spectrum.

Grit, R. (2000). *Informatiemanagement*. Groningen: Wolters-Noordhoff.

Grit, R. (2008). *Zo maak je een informatieplan*. Groningen: Wolters-Noordhoff.

Grit, R. (2008). *Zo maak je een ondernemingsplan*. Groningen: Wolters-Noordhoff.

Grit, R. & Gerritsma, M.J.A. (2007). *Competent adviseren*. Groningen: Wolters-Noordhoff.

Grit, R. & Gerritsma, M. (2008). *Zo organiseer je een event*. Groningen: Noordhoff Uitgevers.

Grit, R. & Gerritsma, M. (2009). *Zo maak je een beleidsplan*. Groningen: Noordhoff Uitgevers.

Grit, R., Guit, R. & Sijde, N. van der (2004). *Competentiemanagement*. Groningen: Wolters-Noordhoff.

Grit, R., Guit, R. & Sijde, N. van der (2006). *Sociaal competent*. Groningen: Wolters-Noordhoff.

Grit, R. & Julsing, M. (2009). *Zo doe je een onderzoek*. Groningen: Noordhoff Uitgevers.

Groote, G.P. e.a. (1991). *Projecten leiden*. Utrecht: Het Spectrum (Marka-serie).

Heerkens, G.R. (2002). *Project Management*. New York: McGraw-Hill.

Hoogland, W. (1992). *Rapporteren over rapporteren*. Groningen: Wolters-Noordhoff.

Horst, F. van der (1991). *Effectief presenteren*. Baarn: Nelissen.

Hulshof, M. (1992). *Leren interviewen*. Groningen: Wolters-Noordhoff.

Kor, R. (1999). *Werken aan projecten*. Deventer: Kluwer.

Luyck, F. (1987). *Vaardig communiceren*. Leiden: Martinus Nijhoff.

Meridith (1985). *Projectmanagement, a managerial approach*. New York: Wiley.

Microsoft (1998). *Microsoft Project 98*. Schoonhoven: Academic Service.

Palm-Hoebé, M. (1989). *Effectieve zakelijke presentaties*. Groningen: Wolters-Noordhoff.

Quinn, R.E. (1997). *Handboek management vaardigheden*. Schoonhoven: Academic Service.

Schermer, M. e.a. (1987). *Vergaderen en onderhandelen*. Alphen aan den Rijn: Samsom.
Steehouder, M. e.a. (1979). *Leren communiceren*. Groningen: Wolters-Noordhoff.
Schein, E., (2001). *De bedrijfscultuur als ziel van de onderneming*. Schiedam: Scriptum.
Sybex (1998). *Werken met Project 98*. Sybex Uitgeverij.
Tumuscheit, K.D. (1998). *Hoe overleef ik een project?* Schiedam: Scriptum.
Verhaar, J. (1996). *Managementvaardigheden voor projectleiders*. Amsterdam: Boom.
Wijnen, G. e.a. (1988). *Projectmatig werken*. Utrecht: Het Spectrum (Marka series).

Magazine on project management
Projectie, published by PMI (i.e. the Project Management Institute), secretariat in Lelystad.

Websites
www.grit-projectmanagement.noordhoff.nl
www.poptoolbox.nl
www.pmtoolbox.nl
www.roelgrit.nl
www.roelgrit.noordhoff.nl
www.noordhoff.nl
www.infoq.nl/projectmanagement/
www.infoq.nl/informatiemanagement/
www.pmi-nl.org/
www.pmi.org/
www.projectmanagement.noordhoff.nl
www.zomaakjeeenplan.noordhoff.nl
www.project-manager.com/
www.ipma-nl.nl
www.pmwiki.nl/
www.allpm.com/
projectmanagement.pagina.nl/
www.competentadviseren.noordhoff.nl
www.sociaalcompetent.noordhoff.nl
www.competentadviseren.noordhoff.nl
www.sociaalcompetent.noordhoff.nl

About the Author

Roel Grit (1954) graduated from Groningen University with a degree in Physical Chemistry and is a bestselling author with Noordhoff Publishers. His publications include the following:
- *Project Management*
- *Information Management*
- *Writing a business plan*
- *Writing an information plan*

The following publications are the result of collaboration with Marco Gerritsma:

- *Zo doe je een risicoanalyse*
- *Zo maak je een beleidsplan*
- *Zo organiseer je een event*
- *Zo maak je een kwaliteitsplan*
- *Zo maak je een personeelsplan*
- *Competent adviseren*

He has also written the following books in collaboration with various other authors:

- *Zo studeer je*   with Saskia Grit
- *Zo doe je een onderzoek*   with Mark Julsing
- *Competentiemanagement*   with Roelie Guit & Nico van der Sijde
- *Sociaal competent*   with Roelie Guit & Nico van der Sijde
- *Management en Logistiek*   with Jan de Geus

More Information on the author can be found at:
- www.roelgrit.noordhoff.nl
- www.roelgrit.nl.

In addition to his part-time activities, Roel is also an instructor at the Stenden Hogeschool in Emmen and co-owner of the company Info/Q automatisering, based in Emmen.

Index